CAPTAIN BUCKO'S
GALLEY SLAVE COOKBOOK

Ahoy! To the best cook on land
or sea, I salute ye. Better make
it good or you'll walk the
plank and then I'll sick the
Kracken on you...

Cap'tain Laura Davey-Jones-
Where's-The-Rum Galijan

ALSO BY ROGER PAUL HUFF

- *Captain Bucko's Nauti-Words Handbook*, Fascinating Facts and Fables About the Origins of Hundreds of Nautical Terms and Everyday Expressions.

- *Fresh Earthworms Taste Green (The Early Years)*, Entertaining Short Stories of a Typical Kid Growing Up in Mid-America Among Tombstones, Indian Bones, Pet Skunks, Rhythm Bands, Vindictive Parrots, UFOs, Gigantic Chickens, Love Slaves, and Lollipops.

- *Captain Bucko's Water & Weather Handbook*, An Entertaining and Easy-To-Read Collection of Inside Information, Fascinating Facts, Trivial Tidbits, and Helpful Hints by a Professional Oceanographer and Marine Meteorologist, to Help Make Your Voyages Safer and More Enjoyable.

CAPTAIN BUCKO'S GALLEY SLAVE COOKBOOK

Fascinating Facts, Sea Stories, & 100+ Famous Recipes From Worldwide Ports Of Call

Roger Paul Huff

iUniverse, Inc.
New York Lincoln Shanghai

CAPTAIN BUCKO'S GALLEY SLAVE COOKBOOK
Fascinating Facts, Sea Stories,
& 100+ Famous Recipes From Worldwide Ports Of Call

Copyright © 2007 by Write Aweigh

iUniverse books may be ordered through booksellers or by contacting:

iUniverse
2021 Pine Lake Road, Suite 100
Lincoln, NE 68512
www.iuniverse.com
1-800-Authors (1-800-288-4677)

Front Cover Artwork by Thomas Rowlandson, 1799

ISBN: 978-0-595-44537-0 (pbk)
ISBN: 978-0-595-88865-8 (ebk)

Printed in the United States of America

To My Very Tasteful Friends and Shipmates

Contents

ACKNOWLEDGEMENTS

I wish to thank: the Bay Breeze Bed & Breakfast, Chef Peter Brinckerhoff, Jim and Sabina Cottrell, Mike Ginsberg, Chef Lee Kresy, Master Chef Stephen Lo, Maw Maw, the Louis Pappas Restaurant, the Royal Navy, Chef Chris and Nick Sarlas, the United States Navy, the Vanilla Queen, Visitor/ Tourist Bureaus of Alabama, Alaska, Andalusia, the Bahamas, Boston, Florida, Georgia, Hawaii, Jamaica, Louisiana, Memphis, Minnesota, Mississippi, Monterey County, New Orleans, St. Louis, Samoa, and Tahiti; plus all of the other organizations and individuals who very graciously contributed inputs to this unique cookbook.

I also want to personally thank: J. Stacey Andrews and Gary Fuis, Carol and Jesse Couch, Pete and Jan Delcour, Linda and Gary Dunham, Gene and Gail Harvey, my wife Janet, Nancy and Bill Keswick, Judy and Lew Lewis, Tom and Susie Moore, Chef Marlies and Allen Pendarvis, C.W. and Gina Rogers, Kathy Seidel, and Larry and Carolyn Williams; who courageously tried many of these recipes. Without their intestinal fortitude, this book would have been tasteless.

PREFACE

Landlubber's cookbooks are boring! They contain a bunch of recipes for dishes like meatloaf or green bean casserole, and reading one after the other is slightly less exciting than watching concrete cure. Those of us who go down to the seas in ships, lakes in launches, rivers on rafts, bayous in boats, and ponds in punts are a lot more adventurous and inquisitive! We want to know where our recipes originated, and the stories behind them. That is why *Captain Bucko's Galley Slave Cookbook* includes: fascinating facts, sea stories, and famous recipes from around the world; and even answers that centuries-old landlubber's question of,

"Why is a vessel's kitchen called a galley?"

The term galley was originally used to describe a vessel propelled mainly by oars, although some were also equipped with sails. During ancient times, galleys were employed by the Phoenicians, Greeks, Romans, and others. The advent of lateen (fore and aft) sails ended the use of galleys for commerce, but the Italian, French, Spanish, and other navies continued to use them for centuries afterward[1] because oars offered more reliable speed and maneuverability. It is estimated that a 120-foot long galley with a single bank of 25 oarsmen on each side could reach a speed of about nine knots, which is just a knot or so slower than modern racing rowboats. That's nice, but

"Why is a vessel's kitchen called a galley?"

---

1.   The infamous Captain Kidd sailed in a galley, but it did not have one onboard. In America, galleys were used during the *Battle of Valcour Island* as late as 1776.

So who rowed the galleys? The answer may surprise you. In the earlier designs where each rower was solely responsible for managing one oar, rowing required some skill and was performed by trained volunteers. If it became necessary to use slaves back then, they were often freed and trained first. However, when later galleys used more rowers on each oar, individual skills did not matter as much and it became common to use prisoners of war or condemned criminals. These so-called galley slaves were sometimes branded with the letters "G.A.L.," and Louis XIV once ordered French courts to sentence convicts to the galleys as frequently as possible to increase the size of his fleet. Galleys were eventually replaced by the "man-of-war," an ocean-going fighting ship heavily armed with cannon and using advanced sails that could tack into the wind. Galley slaves were sent to prisons ashore, but were still called *galerien* (France) and *galera* (Spain) until into the 19th century. All of this history is very interesting, but

"Why is a vessel's kitchen called a galley?"

I am so glad you finally asked this! Some say that it came from the use of galley slaves as cooks. Others maintain the term was derived from the brick or stone "gallery" area amidships where sailors cooked their meals. So, now you know

"Why a vessel's kitchen is called a galley."

I have only been boating for just over half a century, so I still have a lot to learn. After being raised on the Mississippi, I spent my college years on and under the waters of the Florida Keys and the Bahamas before my 21-year stint in the Navy took me from the Mediterranean to Micronesia. I consumed some strange things along the way, many of which I subsequently decided were inedible. I wanted to share some of these treasured recipes before they drifted off into the fog bank of my memories. Some are rather old and rare, while others are more modern. All come from (more or less) exotic ports of call, and most have great stories to tell.

—**Captain Bucko**

INTRODUCTION

Most of us never give much thought to how water has shaped world history. It opened trade routes and led to discovery of the New World. Oceans insulated fledgling colonies from foreign subjugation, and helped many of them achieve independence. Great lakes and rivers provided sources of food and routes for exploration, transportation, and trade. Throughout history, water has had a major effect upon where we live, how we travel, and what we eat.

Since navigation was in its infancy, during ancient times most voyages took place within sight of land ... and when it came to provisioning, this practice had certain advantages. Crews could fish in the shallow waters, and went ashore to procure fresh food and water as long as the locals were friendly. But when Columbus set sail on the third day of August in 1492, one of the principal challenges that faced the 88 souls aboard his three small ships was where and how they were going to replenish their supplies of food, wine, and water.

The diets of Spanish mariners back then included water, wine, cheese, raisins, rice, nuts, honey, molasses, ship's biscuits, dried chickpeas and beans, pickled or salted fish and meats, vinegar, garlic, and salted flour. Most of the provisions were stored in wooden casks, which often let the preserving brine leak out of the casks of meat and let moisture leak into those that held dry provisions. Salting methods had become relatively good by then, and properly prepared meat could keep up to 40 years provided the casks were kept in good order and the contents were not allowed to dry out. Ship's biscuits (a.k.a. hardtack) might last a year or longer if kept dry, but they had to be soaked awhile to become soft enough to eat.

Sailors drank water and wine stored in wooden barrels, and the latter was very high in alcohol content, which helped preserve it. This must have made quite an impression on Columbus, because when he left on his next voyage his ships were ballasted with barrels of Spanish wine instead of rocks. *Captain Bucko's Galley Slave Cookbook* includes some authentic recipes from back then, but you might not want to serve some of these dishes at the Commodore's next dinner party!

Things did not improve quickly for honest mariners aboard naval and merchant vessels, and their weekly rations often looked something like the following:

> Two pounds of salt pork
> Two pints of dried peas
> Three pints of oatmeal
> Four pounds of salt beef
> Six ounces of (rancid) butter
> Seven pounds of (infested) hardtack
> Seven gallons of beer, wine, or spirits
> Twelve ounces of (bone hard) cheese

The best nautical cuisine during the 17th and early 18th centuries might have been aboard vessels of privateers and pirates, simply because they were less committed to bureaucratic regimen and more opportunistic. While crews of merchant and naval vessels ate salted meat, dried peas, and moldy hardtack; whenever pirates ran short of decent food they would raid the stores of other vessels or go ashore to replenish their supplies. There were wild onions, yams, bananas, plantains, papayas, pineapples, dates, and guava. Pirates hunted wild boar, goats, monkeys, birds, and turtles; and some of them earned an unusual nickname because of their culinary habits. French explorers learned that West Indies natives smoked meat upon racks called *boucans*, so they called pirates of the Caribbean *boucaniers* ... and that nickname finally evolved into *buccaneers*.

Most pirate vessels did not carry that much water, because it quickly became undrinkable. Many drank beer, wine, *bumboo* made out of rum, water, nutmeg, and sugar, and *rumfustian* (a combination of raw eggs, sugar, sherry, gin, and beer). Diets of honest seamen during the 19th Century remained pretty bland, boring, and not very healthy. Rum was about the only bright spot in the daily routine of Royal Navy sailors, until a stodgy Admiral watered it down into grog!

Fire onboard has long been a concern, and another advantage to remaining in coastal waters was the ability to do least some cooking ashore. As previously mentioned, early galleys cooked on brick or stone platforms located away from flammable items. By the time of Columbus, these had evolved into fireboxes called "fogons," although foul weather and blowing sparks remained problems. Later vessels such as the *USS Constitution* had wood-fired "cambooses" which doubled as cooking stoves and forges. This was also the only area below deck where crewmembers were allowed to smoke tobacco. These days boaters still cook over everything from charcoal briquettes in the bottom of a perforated tomato juice can to fancy stainless steel grills fueled by propane.

According to *Captain Bucko's Nauti-Words Handbook*, the ship's stovepipe was nicknamed "Charlie Noble," and a very common seasoning for many dishes was "galley pepper" (i.e., black soot from ol' Charlie Noble). Meals were often cooked in communal pots and served upon square wooden plates. The latter were easier to stow than round ones, and led to the common expression "a square meal."

Captain Bucko's Galley Slave Cookbook contains rare and famous recipes from ports of call on oceans, lakes, rivers, and bayous around the world. Some are old, some are traditional, some are modern, and some of them even come from the Golden Age of Piracy. So the next time that any of you galley slaves out there are called upon to cater a boarding party or face a surly crew that is lobbying for lobscouse, hollering for hardtack, or mutinying for mead; I hope you will refer to this book before you get flogged!

BOARDING PARTIES

With possible exception of the words that, "The Captain wants to go waterskiing," very few things strike fear into galley slaves more than unexpected guests. They show up without any warning, rarely bring their own vittles, and their table manners are usually atrocious. If you are occasionally faced with such events, here are some recipes to satiate even the rowdiest of boarders.

ARMADILLO EGGS (GALVESTON, TX)

Texans say that the chicken crossed the road just to show the armadillo that it could be done. Armadillos cannot see or hear very well, and they look a lot like possums in full body armor. The reason that they are included in this nautical cookbook is that they were the secret weapons in a maritime attack that Spain launched against England in 1588. The *Spanish Armadillada* was unsuccessful however, because most of the little rascals drowned while trying to swim across the Channel. The survivors tiptoed to Texas and founded the city of *Armadillo*.

Wha' Cha' Need:

Mixing bowl
Deep fryer

16 Jalapeño peppers
One cup of grated jack cheese
Two eggs
¼ cup of milk
½ cup of flour
One cup of seasoned bread crumbs
Two cups of safflower oil

Wha' Cha' Do:

Wash and dry the peppers thoroughly to remove as much wax or oil from their skins as possible, then cut off their tops and remove the membranes and seeds. Stuff each pepper with the grated cheese and set them aside. Blend the eggs and milk together. Dust the peppers with the flour, gently dip them into the egg/milk mixture, and set them aside to dry for approximately ten minutes. Next dredge them in the breadcrumbs and tenderly place them into the freezer for about two hours. Heat up the safflower oil to 370 degrees F and fry the eggs until they are golden brown, but do not let your pet armadillo watch you do this! Drain them well on paper towels and let them cool just a little before serving.

CEVICHE (MEXICO)

Yuppies use it as a dip for Fritos while swilling designer tequila, but ceviche (also spelled seviche or cebiche) is actually a centuries-old dish. Some say that it was introduced to South America by Arabian immigrants, but it may have originated with ancient Incan civilizations of modern-day Peru or Ecuador. There are many regional variations. In Peru, it is served with corn on the cob or slices of chilled sweet potatoes. In Ecuador, it may be served in crystal bowls or pastry shells, accompanied by nuts, potato chips, corn nuts, or even popcorn. In Mexico, it often contains onions and tomatoes, and is served upon tortilla chips. In any case, it is essentially seafood that has been "cooked" using acidic citrus juice instead of any heat, so get away from that stove! Here is one ceviche recipe.

Wha' Cha' Need:

Non-metallic mixing bowl

One pound of seafood (shrimp, scallops, white fish)
One and ½ cup of fresh limejuice
Two minced Serrano peppers
One medium onion, chopped
One medium tomato, skinned & cubed
Six tablespoons of olive oil
Two tablespoons of white wine vinegar
¼ teaspoon of oregano
½ teaspoon of fresh ground black pepper
½ teaspoon of salt
Lime wedges

Wha' Cha' Do:

Clean and rinse any fish, pat it dry, remove the skin and bones, then shred it. Shell and de-vein the shrimp. Place all of the seafood into a non-metallic bowl, cover it completely with the limejuice, and refrigerate for at least two hours. Stir it well then drain off the limejuice. After mixing the peppers, onion, tomato, olive oil, white wine vinegar, oregano, black pepper, and salt together, combine it with the seafood, thoroughly coating the latter. Some native fishermen next bury it in the sand, but less adventurous (and more sanitary) types should refrigerate it for at least three hours. Bring the mixture to room temperature before serving, and garnish it with lime wedges. Serves four.

Note—The remaining juice is called "tiger's milk," and it is said to be an excellent remedy for a hangover from drinking too much of that designer tequila. But you can also mix it with vodka or Pisco (a grape brandy from Peru).

CRAB CAKES (CHESAPEAKE BAY)

Combining minced meat with fillers and spices has been done for centuries as a way to add flavor and make the meat go further. Although this traditional dish dates back to Colonial America, it was formerly called "crab croquettes" or "crab patties." The term "crab cake" first appeared during the 1930s in the *New York World's Fair Cookbook,* … but if you eat one on a bun it's called a "crab burger."

Wha' Cha' Need:

Two mixing bowls
Sauté pan or broiler

One pound of crabmeat
One egg
One teaspoon of lemon juice
One teaspoon of seafood seasoning
One teaspoon of Worcestershire sauce
One teaspoon of parsley flakes
¼ teaspoon of dry mustard
One heaping tablespoon of mayonnaise
One heaping teaspoon of prepared mustard
¼ cup of cracker crumbs or breadcrumbs
Two tablespoons of extra virgin olive oil

Wha' Cha' Do:

Put the crabmeat into a bowl (are you with me so far?). In another bowl combine the egg, lemon juice, seafood seasoning, Worcestershire sauce, parsley flakes, dry mustard, mayonnaise, and prepared mustard. Add the cracker or breadcrumbs to this mixture, and fold it into the crabmeat, being careful not to break up the latter. Shape the mixture into slightly flattened patties and chill. Either sauté the cakes in olive oil or broil them until they are golden brown on both sides. Drain and serve hot. The number of cakes that this recipe yields depends upon their size, which clearly proves that size is important … at least among crabs!

FRENCH FRIED ZUCCHINI (LAKE TAHOE, CA)

A popular stop for boaters on Tahoe's West Shore is the *Sunnyside Restaurant & Lodge*, located on the parcel where Captain Kendrick (the founder of the Schlage Lock Company) built his summer estate back in 1908. Their lakefront deck and "Old Tahoe" décor attract guests year-round, and their signature appetizer is undoubtedly their French fried zucchini. Here's the recipe, courtesy of Chef Lee.

Wha' Cha' Need:

Shallow pan
Mixing bowl
Deep fryer

The Breading:
Cracker meal
Coarse breadcrumbs
Regular breadcrumbs

The Dish:
One pound of whole zucchini
One whole egg
Five ounces of buttermilk
Five ounces of whole milk
Flour
Cooking Oil
Ranch Dressing

Wha' Cha' Do:

The Breading:
Combine equal parts of the cracker meal, coarse breadcrumbs, and regular breadcrumbs in a shallow pan, and set this mixture aside.

The Dish:

Wash the zucchini in cold water, and cut off both ends. Cut it in half, then slice each half lengthwise into ¼ inch sticks. Combine the egg, buttermilk, and whole milk in a bowl. Dredge the zucchini sticks first in the flour, then in this egg/milk mixture, and finally in the breading mixture. Deep-fry them in 350 degree F oil until they are golden brown. Drain well, and serve with Ranch dressing. Makes one serving.

FRIED DILL PICKLES (LONG BEACH, MS)

I originally encountered these culinary curiosities at a mom-and-pop fried (isn't everything?) chicken stand on Mississippi's Gulf Coast. They were listed on the wall menu in between the fried alligator and fried chicken gizzards. Their origin may have been lost in the mists of antiquity, but most food archeologists agree that they were invented sometime after the invention of sliced pickles, which occurred shortly after the invention of the pickle-slicer, which probably took place after the pickle was invented. However, they could all be wrong!

Wha' Cha' Need:

Large glass mixing bowl
Deep fryer or large saucepan

One cup of all-purpose flour
¼ cup of cornstarch
One teaspoon of baking powder
¼ teaspoon of salt
One cup of ice water
One egg yolk
Two tablespoons of dill pickle juice
Four cups of drained dill pickle slices
Vegetable oil for frying

Wha' Cha' Do:

In a large bowl, combine the flour, cornstarch, baking powder, and salt. Make a well in the center of this dry mixture. Add the water, egg yolk, and pickle juice and stir the mixture with a wire whisk to make a smooth batter. Cover the bowl and refrigerate for 30 minutes. Heat at least two inches of oil to 375 degrees F in a deep fryer or a large saucepan. Dip batches of the pickle slices into the batter, coating them evenly but lightly. Without crowding them (Hey!), carefully place the batter-coated pickle slices into the hot oil (Ouch!) Fry them until they are golden and crisp, about 1½ to 2 minutes. Drain well and serve.

MARGARITA CHICKEN WINGS (MEXICO)

Those of you whose minds are cluttered with completely worthless information already know that Buffalo Wings were created in the *Anchor Bar* in Buffalo, NY, but the question of where the Margarita was invented is not as easily answered. Some say that a bartender in Juarez whipped it up from Tequila, Cointreau, and limejuice because he couldn't remember how to make a "Magnolia" ordered by a lady customer. Others claim that a Virginia City, NV bartender named the first one after his girlfriend, who hit someone over the head with a whiskey bottle and died in the ensuing gunfight. Some say it was created for actress Rita Hayworth, while others maintain that a Margarita Sames invented the drink (and modestly named it after herself) for a party she threw in Acapulco. The following recipe blends the taste of the original Buffalo Wings with the mysterious Margarita.

Wha' Cha' Need:

Large re-sealable plastic bag
Small glass mixing bowl
Charcoal grill
Charcoal

Two pounds of chicken wings, cut into two pieces
½ cup of gold tequila or mescal
¼ cup of frozen orange juice concentrate
Grated zest of one lemon
Juice of one lemon
Two cloves of garlic, minced
½ teaspoon of ground cumin
One teaspoon of coarsely ground black pepper
One teaspoon of salt
Two tablespoons of minced cilantro

Wha' Cha' Do:

Wash the wings, pat them dry and place them into a large heavy-duty re-sealable plastic bag. In a small bowl, combine all of the remaining ingredients and pour the mixture over the wings in the bag. Seal the bag and refrigerate it for several hours or overnight. Prepare a medium-hot charcoal fire or pre-heat a gas grill to medium heat. Drain the wings and discard the marinade. Grill them, turning often, until they are slightly charred and cooked through, about 25 minutes. Serves four.

PIÑA COLADA SHRIMP (PUERTO RICO)

Some folks say that the Piña Colada was created to get rid of a surplus of stupid little paper umbrellas. However, this very popular drink was actually invented by a Spaniard named Ricardo Gracias while he was working as bar manager at the Caribé Hilton Hotel in San Juan, Puerto Rico. Back in 1954, their hotel guests were provided a complimentary drink called a "Coco Loco" that was served in a freshly cut coconut shell. One day all their coconut cutters went on strike, so Ricardo had to come up another container. Luckily, he noticed that the hotel had a large supply of fresh pineapples, so he cut off their tops and filled them with Coco-Loco. After he later improved the taste by adding crushed ice and strained pineapple, he called it a "Piña Colada." If you like Piña Coladas and shrimp, you will probably like the following recipe, courtesy of Señor Gracias:

Wha' Cha' Need:

Four mixing bowls
Vegetable oil
Deep fryer

The Dish:
One cup of cornstarch
One cup of liquid (non-alcoholic) piña colada drink mix
Two tablespoons of powdered sugar
1/3 cup of spiced rum
Two cups of plain breadcrumbs
Two cups of sweetened coconut flakes
One pound of jumbo shrimp, peeled, de-veined, and butterflied

The Dipping Sauce:
½ cup of liquid (non-alcoholic) piña colada drink mix
1/3 cup of sour cream
1/3 cup of crushed pineapple, drained

Wha Cha' Do:

Set aside one cup of cornstarch in a bowl. In a separate bowl, combine one cup of the (non-alcoholic) piña colada drink mix, powdered sugar, and spiced rum, and set it aside also. Combine the breadcrumbs and coconut flakes in a third bowl, and mix up the dipping sauce in a fourth bowl. Coat the shrimp in the cornstarch, dip them into the piña colada drink mix/sugar/rum mixture, then into the breadcrumb/coconut mixture, back once more into the piña colada drink mix/sugar/rum mixture, and back again into the breadcrumb/coconut mixture. Carefully drop each of the coated shrimp into 375 degree F oil, and fry them until they are golden brown. Drain before serving and dip away, matey!

POISSON CRU (TAHITI)

This is not a recipe for poisoning the crew, but if the fish that you use is not very fresh the result may be the same. Poisson is French for fish, while a *poissonnier* is a fishmonger. This is one of the most famous traditional dishes of Tahiti, and some people think of it as Polynesian ceviche. I will let you decide for yourself.

Wha' Cha' Need:

Two glass mixing bowls

One pound of fresh Ahi tuna, diced
1/3 cup of fresh lemon/limejuice
Salt and pepper to taste
½ to one teaspoon of (Tahitian) vanilla extract
½ cup of coconut milk (fresh preferred)
½ cup of carrots, shredded
½ cup of scallions, thinly sliced
½ cup of tomatoes, diced,
½ cup of cucumber, diced small
½ cup of red bell pepper, diced small
Parsley or chives for garnish
Sliced cherry tomatoes for garnish

Wha' Cha' Do:

Mix the tuna and the lemon/limejuice together with salt and pepper. Let this mixture marinate for several minutes, or until the tuna looks "cooked." Mix the vanilla with the coconut milk, and combine with the other ingredients. Season to taste, and garnish with parsley, chives, and sliced cherry tomatoes. Serves four.

SAGANAKI (GREECE)

The name of this dish is not a misspelling of a Japanese city, but is derived from the name of the pan (i.e., *sagani*) in which it is traditionally prepared. In Greece variations include shrimp or chicken, but in the United States saganaki usually refers to an appetizer made out of slices of mild cheese like Fontinella or Kasseri that are dusted in flour, shallow-fried, and sprinkled with lemon juice. A Greek restaurateur in the Chicago area began to flame the traditional dish with brandy just before serving, and this presentation usually results in a resounding "Opa!"

Wha' Cha' Need:

Heavy skillet
Mixing bowl

Four tablespoons of butter
One egg, well beaten
One teaspoon of flour
½ pound of (Fontinella or Kasseri) cheese
Two tablespoons of brandy
Juice of ½ a lemon

Wha' Cha' Do:

Heat the butter in a heavy skillet over moderate heat. Cut the cheese into slices that are roughly ½ inch thick. Beat the egg and the flour together in a bowl and dip the cheese slices into this mixture. Next place the slices into the skillet and fry them until they are well browned on both sides. Remove the skillet from the heat and add the brandy. Carefully ignite the brandy, and move the skillet until the flame is extinguished. Squeeze the lemon juice over the cheese and serve it from the skillet along with crusty (Pita or French) bread. *Opa!*

TOASTED RAVIOLI (ST. LOUIS, MO)

Riverboats used to tie up along the banks of the Mississippi in front of where the 630-foot tall stainless steel *Gateway Arch* now stands. Legend says that toasted ravioli originated back in 1947, when a cook at Angelo's restaurant accidentally dropped some freshly made ravioli into breadcrumbs and decided to fry them up rather than throw them out. In the Midwest, toasted ravioli are usually stuffed with beef or veal, but in New England they may contain provolone or Parmesan cheese. There are even rumors of chicken-filled ones in western states.

Wha' Cha' Need:

Two shallow mixing bowls
Deep fryer

Two tablespoons of condensed milk
One large egg, lightly beaten
¾ cup of dry Italian-seasoned breadcrumbs
One teaspoon of salt (optional)
½ of a (27½ ounce) package of frozen ravioli, thawed
Vegetable oil for frying
Grated Parmesan cheese
Marinara or pizza sauce

Wha' Cha' Do:

Combine the milk and egg in a small bowl. Place the breadcrumbs and salt into a shallow bowl. Dip the individual ravioli into the milk mixture, then coat with breadcrumbs. Fry the ravioli a few at a time in two inches of oil heated to 375 degrees F about one minute on each side until golden brown. Drain, sprinkle them with grated Parmesan cheese, and serve immediately with warmed marinara or pizza sauce. Serves four Goombas.

FOR CHOWDERHEADS

Some say that the word chowder originated with the Latin word *calderia*, which meant "a place to warm things." From calderia came the word cauldron, and in French this was *chaudiere*. When early fishing vessels returned home townsfolk had large chaudieres waiting for some of their catch to be cooked and served as part of their homecoming celebrations. Here are chowder recipes and more.

CALLALOO (TRINIDAD & TOBAGO)

Callaloo is the national dish of Trinidad & Tobago (T&T), but is sometimes called "pepper pot" in Jamaica and Guyana. It can be served as a soup, a side dish, or as gravy for other food, and its color comes from leafy green vegetables. Recipes vary throughout the West Indies, but most of them, include okra, coconut milk, hot pepper, and sometimes crab, lobster, or other meat. Local legend says that feeding a man Callaloo will make him propose, so be careful out there!

Wha' Cha' Need:

Large heavy saucepan

One pound of callaloo, spinach, or Swiss chard leaves
Six cups of chicken stock
One onion, finely chopped
One clove of garlic, chopped
Three whole scallions, chopped
¼ teaspoon of thyme
Four ounces of lean salt pork cut into ½-inch cubes
½ pound of fresh, canned, or frozen crabmeat
½ cup of coconut milk
½ pound of fresh or 10 ounce package of frozen okra, sliced
Salt and pepper to taste
Hot pepper sauce to taste

Wha' Cha' Do:

Wash the greens, remove the stems and heavy veins, and coarsely chop up the leaves. Put the chopped leaves into a large heavy saucepan with the chicken stock, onion, garlic, scallions, thyme, and salt pork. Cover and cook it at a gentle simmer until the pork is tender. Add the crabmeat, coconut milk, and okra. Cook until the okra is done or about ten minutes. Season it to taste with salt, pepper, and hot pepper sauce. Serves six.

Note—Callaloo soup is often served with *foo-foo*, green plantains that have been boiled, pounded into balls, and seasoned.

CATAPLANA (PORTIMAO, PORTUGAL)

Moors ruled the Algarve coast of medieval Portugal for over six centuries, during the time that alchemists vainly tried to turn base metal into gold by heating it in an enclosed retort. The origin of the word *cataplana* is uncertain, but it is used for this local dish as well as for the primitive pressure cooker in which it is traditionally prepared. The latter is an airtight copper pot that looks a bit like a football that has been cut in half and has hinges on one side. But even if there is no cataplana in your cupboard, you can still make this unique seafood stew.

Wha' Cha' Need:

Cataplana or wide saucepan with a tight-fitting lid

Eight ounces of fresh small clams (in shell), scrubbed
Eight ounces of fresh mussels (in shell), scrubbed
Eight ounces of raw prawns (in shell)
Eight ounces of squid tube rings
Four fluid ounces of white wine
Four cloves of garlic, chopped
Eight sprigs of fresh thyme
One bay leaf
Two ounces of extra virgin olive oil

Wha' Cha' Do:

Put all of the ingredients in the bottom of a wide saucepan with a tight fitting lid. Place the pan over a low to medium heat, cover it with the lid and cook for five to eight minutes until the clam and mussel shells have steamed open. Stir well, discard any mussels or clams that have not opened, and serve immediately. Serves four.

CIOPPINO (SAN FRANCISCO, CA)

Some say that the name for San Francisco's most famous seafood stew is derived from the Italian word *ciuppin,* but most agree that the dish itself likely originated with the Genoese fishermen who settled in northern California. It was relatively unknown beyond the Bay until after World War II, but has become as traditional as the cable cars, Ghirardelli Square, and the fog that rolls in through the Golden Gate. Cioppino recipes vary, but it is basically seafood stew that often includes: (Dungeness) crab, clams, shrimp or prawns, squid, sometimes the fish catch of the day, a basic sauce of tomatoes, garlic, and spices, and a splash of wine. It is frequently served with warm San Francisco Sourdough bread, and it is delicious.

Wha' Cha' Need:

Large heavy pot
Serving bowls

Two tablespoons of olive oil
One large onion, chopped
Three cloves of garlic, crushed or to taste
Two (28 ounce) cans of diced tomatoes with juice
½ cup of dry white wine
¼ cup of chopped fresh parsley
½ teaspoon of dried basil
Two teaspoons of salt
½ teaspoon of cracked black pepper
One bay leaf
One pound of scallops
24 littleneck clams
One and ½ pounds of (Dungeness) crab legs
One pound of unpeeled, large fresh shrimp

Wha' Cha' Do:

Heat the olive oil in a large heavy pot over medium-high heat. Add the onion and garlic, and cook until they are soft, stirring frequently. Pour in the tomatoes and white wine, and season with parsley, basil, salt, pepper and the bay leaf. Reduce the heat to medium-low, and simmer it for about an hour. Next add the scallops, clams, crab legs, and shrimp to the pot. Cover and cook over medium heat until the clams open, and discard any of them that refuse to do so. Dip portions into large bowls and serve with warm sourdough bread. Serves six. *Mangia!*

CONCH CHOWDER (THE BAHAMAS)

Unless you happen to be a native Bahamian, the most difficult part of this dish might be removing, cleaning, and skinning the conchs. They can also be rather tough, so unless you like eating hockey pucks you may want to consider putting the meat into a sturdy plastic freezer bag with a little bit of vinegar and pounding it mercilessly with some heavy blunt instrument. Even if you really hate seafood, this can be an excellent way to release pent up aggressions.

Wha' Cha' Need:

Tools to remove conch
Cooking pot
Sauté pan

One ham bone, or ¼ to ½ pound of bacon, cubed
Two quarts of water
Meat of eight to ten conchs, cleaned and diced
Two onions, chopped
One green pepper, diced
One can of tomatoes
Six large potatoes, diced
One (6 ounce) can of tomato paste
Salt and pepper to taste
Two to four bay leaves
Two to four tablespoons of thyme
Two tablespoons of butter or margarine
Two to four carrots, sliced
Cayenne pepper or hot sauce to taste

Wha' Cha' Do:

Place the ham bone (or bacon) into a cooking pot and add the water. Cover and bring it to a boil. Turn the heat down to simmer. Add diced the conch meat and simmer for about two hours or until the conch is tender. Sauté the onion, green pepper, and diced potatoes until lightly browned; stirring to prevent burning. Add in the tomatoes and the tomato paste and simmer for another minute of so. Add this mixture into the pot with the conch. Add the remaining ingredients and simmer until the vegetables are cooked.

DOWN EAST CHOWDAH (PENOBSCOT BAY, ME)

Many early chowder recipes included salt pork and ship's biscuits, but crackers have usually replaced the latter today. Folks who live on one side of Penobscot Bay prefer their clam chowder made with tomatoes, whereas those living on the other side like theirs made with milk and no tomatoes. This vital issue became so controversial that in 1939 a state legislator introduced a bill to make it illegal to add tomatoes. Maine chowder is sometimes also called "Down East," because vessels coming from Boston typically had to sail downwind to reach Maine. No matter what you call it, here is a recipe worth trying:

Note—This is not the glutinous mass foisted upon unwitting tourists these days as so-called "New England" or "Boston" clam chowder. This is the real stuff!

Wha' Cha' Need:

Mixing bowl
Re-sealable plastic bag
Heavy four-pint soup kettle

The Spice Blend:
One tablespoon of all-purpose flour
Four teaspoons of dried parsley
Four teaspoons of rosemary
Four teaspoons of oregano
Four teaspoons of thyme
Four teaspoons of basil
Two teaspoons of marjoram
Two teaspoons of tarragon
Two teaspoons of dill
One teaspoon of sage

The Chowdah:
One slice of hickory-smoked bacon, minced
½ teaspoon of butter
One cup of onion, minced
One medium garlic clove, minced
One teaspoon of spice blend (see above)
One (6½ ounce) can of clams
One tablespoon of all-purpose flour
One cup of bottled clam juice
One and ½ cups of half-and-half
¼ teaspoon of ground white pepper
Two medium potatoes, boiled, peeled and diced

Wha' Cha' Do:

The Spice Blend:
Thoroughly mix together all of the spice blend ingredients together. Place the mixture into a re-sealable plastic bag and refrigerate until ready to use. This recipe makes more than you need, so save the remainder for future use.

The Chowdah:
Sauté the bacon, butter, onion, garlic and one teaspoon of the spice blend over low heat in a heavy-bottomed, four-pint soup kettle, but do not allow it to brown. Drain the clams and set them aside, but reserve their juice. Slowly stir the flour and the clam juices into the sauté mixture. Bring to a boil, and reduce the heat. Add the half-and-half, and simmer for 20 more minutes. Add the white pepper, potatoes and clams. Heat it to serving temperature, but do not allow mixture to boil, because this toughens the clams. Serve at once with crackers and warm cornbread. Serves six.

FISH BOIL-OVER (DOOR COUNTY, WI)

Door County lies on a peninsula that is bounded by Lake Michigan on one side and Green Bay on the other. It was a landing for French trappers and traders, and the area was once so wild that it was nicknamed "Death's Door." For more than a century locals have held fish boils to raise funds for community projects, and they have turned into tourist attractions. Early recipes called for trout, but these days mild-flavored local whitefish is more plentiful. Most ingredients are fairly basic, but the final cooking stage can get quite dramatic. Are you ready?

Wha' Cha' Need:

A kettle or sturdy pot with a stand (e.g., a turkey fryer)
A wood fire (away from flammable objects and people)
A little kerosene
Fire extinguishers

Two gallons of water
½ pound of salt
16 small red potatoes
16 small white onions
16 whitefish steaks (two inches thick)

Wha' Cha' Do:

After adding ¼ pound of salt to the two gallons of water in the kettle/pot, light the wood fire and bring the mixture to a boil. Cut the ends off of the potatoes, add them to the kettle/pot, and boil for 15 minutes. Peel the white onions, add them to the kettle/pot, and boil for four more minutes. Add the fish steaks and other ¼ pound of salt, and boil for another ten minutes. As the finishing touch, very carefully throw a little kerosene onto the fire to cause a boil-over to remove the fish oil and other impurities. Drain the mixture through a colander. Serve it with melted butter, lemon wedges, cole slaw, bread, beverages of your choice, and (traditionally) a piece of cherry pie. Serves eight.

Warning—Do not try this recipe at home unless you are a trained professional, a pyromaniac, or a little unbalanced … and have the fire department standing by.

JAMBALAYA (CHALMETTE, LA)

Some say that the weird name for this dish was derived from the combination of *jambon* (French for ham), *a la* (French for "in the style of"), and *ya* (West African for rice). A more colorful legend says that the name came from when a hungry traveler arrived at the *New Orleans Inn* after the kitchen had already closed for the evening. The host reportedly told Jean, the cook, to *balayez* or "mix some things together," and the guest thought that he had ordered something called "Jean Balayez." Although rice is a main ingredient, recipes may also include: chicken, ham, crawfish, shrimp, smoked (andouille or chorizo) sausage, turtle, alligator, the so-called "Holy Trinity" of onions, celery, and bell peppers, and of course, Tabasco.

Wha' Cha' Need:

Large saucepan

One pound of Louisiana hot links, sliced
One large onion, diced
One cup of bell pepper, diced
One cup of celery, diced
One (28 ounce) can of diced tomatoes
One cup of cocktail sauce
Season with thyme, marjoram
Chili pepper paste
Two cups of rice, cooked
Salt and Tabasco to taste

Wha' Cha' Do:

Combine the sausage, onion, bell pepper, celery, and diced tomatoes in a large saucepan. Simmer for about an hour and then add a little water if needed. Next add the cocktail sauce, and season with thyme, marjoram, and chili pepper paste to taste. Add the cooked rice into the mixture. Cook over low heat for about ten more minutes. Salt to taste and serve. Serves about six. *Laissez Les Bons Temps Rouler!*

LOBSCOUSE (LIVERPOOL, ENGLAND)

European sailors originally brought *labskause* to England, where its name was anglicized to lobscouse. It became so popular in Liverpool that people from that area are sometimes called "Scousers." Most recipes include the same principal ingredients of: meat, vegetables, and potatoes; but a vegetarian version is called "Blind Scouse" for no apparent reason whatsoever. Lobscouse can be prepared, kept covered in the refrigerator for up to two days, and re-heated.

Wha' Cha' Need:

Large cooking pot
Serving bowls

Four tablespoons of butter
One and ½ pounds of beef, cut into one-inch cubes
Three medium onions, chopped
Three cups of beer
Three cups of beef stock (or bullion)
Two bay leaves
One teaspoon of salt
Fresh ground pepper
Six medium potatoes cut into one-inch cubes
Six tablespoons of butter (optional)
Three tablespoons of green onion tops, chopped

Wha' Cha' Do:

Brown the meat and cook the onions together in the butter, stirring occasionally. Add the beer, beef stock, bay leaves, salt, and pepper. Cover and simmer for 20 minutes. Add the potatoes and continue to simmer for two hours. Mash any remaining pieces of potato, so you have thick gravy with just a few pieces of potato. Serve it in bowls with a tablespoon of butter on the top (optional). Sprinkle it with onion tops. Serves six Scousers, or four hungry Beatles.

LOBSTER STEW (PORTLAND, ME)

Lobster was not always considered to be a delicacy touted by the well to do. In colonial New England it was considered as "pauper's food." A pile of lobster shells around a house was viewed as a sign of poverty, and colonists fed them to swine. The swine didn't mind, but some colonists began to get a bit suspicious when they began finding little tubs of drawn lemon butter in more and more pigpens. One reason that lobsters were considered to be so "common" back then was because they were. By dragging a hook through shallow waters, one could easily catch a pail full of them. Lobster salad gained enough respectability to be listed on restaurant menus by the 1850s, but it sold for about half the price of chicken salad. As recently as the 1940s, kids from poorer sections of coastal towns still traded lobster sandwiches for peanut butter and jelly ones. You don't have to fall in love with Old Cape Cod to enjoy this lobster stew, because this recipe comes from Maine.

Wha' Cha' Need:

Pot for steaming lobsters
Large heavy cooking pot

Four fresh live lobsters
Four tablespoons of butter
One pint of heavy cream
One quart of milk
Salt and pepper

Wha' Cha' Do:

To enhance its flavor, prepare lobster stew the day before serving. Steam or boil the lobsters for about 18 minutes. Place the cooked lobsters onto plates to cool and catch the juices. After the lobsters have cooled, pick the meat from them. Remove the green liver (tomalley) and any coral (roe), but do not discard. After the meat has been picked out, sauté the tomalley and the roe in one and one-half tablespoons of butter in a heavy cooking pot for three minutes. Add more butter and some of the lobster meat into the pot, and repeat until all of the lobster meat has been sautéed for five to ten minutes. Add the cream, the reserved juice, and the milk. Simmer it uncovered over low heat for several hours, taking care not to boil. Add salt and pepper to taste. Serves four.

PAELLA (COSTA DEL SOL, SPAIN)

Rice dishes are quite common in eastern Spain, where rice has been culti-vated ever since being introduced by the Moors in the 8th century. The local peasants often prepared their mid-day meals in a two-handled pan they called a "paella." The first versions contained ingredients that were com-mon to the rice-growing regions such as frogs, eels, broad beans, and snails; but the popularity of the dish eventually spread to the coast (thank good-ness) where seafood and other ingredients were prevalent. Tomatoes and peppers from the New World were added much later. Basic components of modern paella include garlic, olive oil, saffron, and short-medium grained Spanish (Valencia) rice. It is a fiesta dish often cooked outdoors in 16 to 18 inch diameter "paellas," but you could use large frying pans or even flat-bottom Woks.

Wha' Cha' Need:

Cooking pot(s)
Mixing cup
A paella, large frying pan, or flat-bottom Wok

One dozen mussels, scrubbed, steamed open
One pound of jumbo shrimp or prawns
Six tablespoons of olive oil
Two pounds of chicken, cut into small pieces
¼ pound of pork, cut into cubes
One green bell pepper, cut into pieces
Two cloves of garlic, crushed
One medium squid, cleaned and cut into rings
One large tomato, peeled, seeded, and chopped
½ cup of fresh-shelled peas
Six to seven cups of water
Two and ½ cups of Spanish rice
½ teaspoon of saffron, crushed
½ teaspoons of ground paprika
Two teaspoons of salt

Freshly ground black pepper
One red pimiento, cut into strips
One lemon, cut into wedges

Wha' Cha' Do:

Scrub the mussels clean, steam them open, and discard all empty or unopened ones. Set the steamed mussels aside, but strain and reserve the liquid. Cook a few unpeeled shrimp to use as a garnish. Drain and set them aside, but reserve this liquid also. Peel the rest of the shrimp and set aside. Heat the olive oil in a paella, a large frying pan, or a flat-bottom Wok; and slowly brown the pieces of chicken and pork. Add the green bell pepper, garlic, squid, tomatoes, and peas. Combine the reserved mussel liquid, shrimp liquid, and water to make six cups, add it to the pan, and bring it to a boil. Stir in the rice and the peeled shrimp. Combine the crushed saffron, paprika, salt, and pepper in a cup; dissolve it in a little water, stir this mixture into the pan, cook it briskly for ten minutes, then reduce the heat. Garnish the dish with the cooked mussels and cooked unpeeled shrimp, top it with the strips of red pimiento, and cook it for another eight to ten minutes without stirring. Add liquid to keep the rice from scorching. Let it rest for five minutes before serving, and garnish with lemon wedges.

SALMAGUNDI (PIRATE STEW)

Some say the strange name of this dish comes from the Italian phrase *salame conditi*, that means "pickled meat," while others insist it was derived from the French word *salmigondis*. The English first corrupted it into Solomon Grundy then incorporated it into the following children's rhyme:

> *Solomon Grundy was born on a Monday,*
> *Christened on Tuesday, Married on Wednesday*
> *Took sick on Thursday, Got worse on Friday,*
> *Died on Saturday, Buried on Sunday,*
> *And that is the end of Solomon Grundy.*

This dish was popular among pirates, who were known culinary opportunists. It is essentially a stew made out of whatever the cook had on hand at the time, and often included salted or pickled meat, anchovies, onions, garlic, and other spices. There is no single recipe for Salmagundi, but here is one that you might want to try if you have the nerve (and the stomach) for it.

Wha' Cha' Need:

Cooking pot or kettle

One pound of corned beef
One pound of pork, goat, bird, etc.
One bottle of cheap red wine
Lard, shortening, or cooking oil
Three large onions, thinly sliced
Four cloves of fresh garlic, crushed
One tin of anchovy filets, mashed
Three pounds of pickled vegetables
Hard-boiled eggs, grapes, olives
Any other spices you have on hand

Wha' Cha' Do:

Marinate the meat in the cheap red wine for as long as you can keep it away from the crew. Hack it into bite-sized chunks, and brown it along with the onions and crushed garlic in hot lard/shortening/oil. Add the mashed anchovies and the pickled vegetables and simmer until it is done. Add whatever spices you like. Serve with hard boiled eggs, grapes, olives, and large amounts of beer, ale, and/or rum. Take some stomach pills, and hope for the best.

SEAFOOD GUMBO (BATON ROUGE, LA)

In 1755, most residents of Britain's colony of Nova Scotia were French-speaking Acadians. This made the British Governor rather nervous because he worried that they might side with the French during a conflict. He avoided this possibility by ordering *The Great Expulsion*. Thousands of the Acadians were rounded up at gunpoint and deported to various locations. Those who ended up in southern Louisiana became known as Cajuns, and soon learned how to cook just about anything that they could catch or step on. Son of a gun, you'll have great fun on the bayou!

Wha' Cha' Need:

Heavy skillet
Large kettle
Serving bowls

One cup of vegetable oil
One cup of flour
Two cups of chopped onions
Eight ribs of celery, chopped
Three cloves of garlic, minced
Eight cups of chicken broth, canned or from base
Two large (28 ounce) cans of tomatoes, diced
Two (10 ounce) packages of frozen okra, sliced & thawed
One pound of crab claws
¼ cup of Worcestershire sauce
One tablespoon of hot sauce
Two large dried bay leaves
½ cup of fresh minced parsley
Two teaspoons of dried leaf thyme

Two teaspoons of dried leaf basil
Two teaspoons of dried leaf oregano
One teaspoon of sage
One teaspoon of pepper
Two pounds of medium shrimp, peeled and de-veined
One quart of oysters, undrained
One pound of crabmeat
One pound of firm white fish filets, cut into 1-inch pieces
Gumbo filé powder (optional)
Hot cooked rice

Wha' Cha' Do:

First, make the roux. Combine the oil and the flour in a heavy skillet; cook over medium heat for 20 minutes, stirring constantly, until the roux is dark. Be very careful to keep the roux from scorching. Stir in the onion, celery, and garlic; and cook for ten minutes, stirring often. Transfer the mixture to a large kettle. Add the chicken broth, tomatoes, okra, crab claws, Worcestershire sauce, hot sauce, bay leaves, parsley, thyme, basil, oregano, sage, and pepper; and simmer for two hours, while stirring occasionally. Add the shrimp, oysters, crabmeat, and fish; and simmer for 10 to 15 minutes. Remove and discard the bay leaves. Sprinkle it with gumbo filé powder (if desired), and serve the gumbo over hot cooked rice.

EATIN' WEEDS

The ancient Greeks and Romans ate raw vegetables and greens dressed with oil, vinegar, and herbs. The word *salade* was derived from the Roman *herba salata*, which meant "salted herb." Hippocrates maintained that it should be eaten first to prepare one's digestive tract for the food course(s) that followed, while others said that the vinegar in the dressing ruined the taste of wine. Dinner salads as we know them today began to appear during the Renaissance, but by the end of the 19th century home economists suggested that mixed greens on a plate were "too messy," and promoted more orderly forms (e.g., the dreaded gelatin mold). Aboard ship, salad ingredients are often determined by the availability of fresh vegetables. The *1944 Navy Cookbook* included a recipe for "tossed salad," but having served on a ship that spent 28 consecutive days each month at sea, I am quite familiar with the typical progression of ingredients. You might enjoy tossed salads for the first several days after a port call, but these often are followed by cabbage, shredded carrots, the dreaded canned beets and onions, and Jell-o.

COLE SLAW (CHESAPEAKE BAY)

Although ancient Romans enjoyed an earlier version of this dish, the name "cole slaw" actually came from the Dutch *kool sla*, which means "cabbage salad." The original was probably served warm, but in England it was commonly called "cold slaw" until the 1860s. Its popularity boomed in the United States right after a New York City delicatessen owner named Richard Hellman (sound familiar?) created and began marketing bottled mayonnaise back in the early 1900s.

Wha' Cha' Need:

Two glass mixing bowls

One and ½ cup of mayonnaise
½ cup of white vinegar
1/3 cup of sugar
One tablespoon of celery seed
Salt and pepper to taste
One head of green cabbage, finely shredded
Two carrots, finely grated

Wha' Cha' Do:

Blend the mayonnaise, vinegar, sugar, celery seed, and salt and pepper to taste, and mix well. In a large bowl, combine the shredded cabbage and carrots. Pour the dressing over the mixture and blend well. Refrigerate until serving.

CRAB LOUIE SALAD (THE WEST COAST)

Trying to pin down the actual origin of this so-called "King of Salads" is virtually impossible. Some folks claim that it was created in Seattle; some say it was San Francisco, while others maintain that it was really Portland, Oregon. Most agree that it began appearing on West Coast menus sometime between 1904 and 1914. Some claim that it was named after King Louis XIV of France who was known for his voracious appetite, while others insist its name came from an anonymous Italian crab fisherman. Or, it could have been named for my late Uncle Louie, but that seems less likely. (Recipe courtesy of Louie … whoever he was.)

Wha' Cha' Need:

Glass mixing bowl
Serving plates

The Dressing:
One cup of mayonnaise
¼ cup of bottled chili sauce
Two tablespoons of green onions, chopped (include some tops)
Two tablespoons of green bell pepper, finely chopped
One tablespoon of freshly squeezed lemon juice
A dash of Tabasco sauce

The Salad:
One pound of Dungeness crabmeat, lumps and claws
One small head of Iceberg or Bibb lettuce
Two ripe red tomatoes cut into wedges
Two hard-boiled eggs cut into wedges

Wha' Cha' Do:

The Dressing:
Whisk all of the dressing ingredients together, reserving some of the green onion slices to use as garnish.

The Salad:

Separate the lettuce leaves, and wash and dry them thoroughly. Make beds of lettuce leaves on four serving plates. Top each with a mound of crabmeat and arrange the tomato and hard-boiled egg wedges around the edge of each plate. Place a spoonful of the dressing on top of each mound of crab-meat, top with a few slices of green onion. Pass remaining dressing at the table. Serves four lunches or light entrees.

Note—You could make similar dishes with king crab, snow crab, or even bay shrimp. But they would not be authentic Crab Louis salads, would they?

GREEN GODDESS DRESSING (SAN FRANCISCO, CA)

This famous dressing was one of the most popular on the West Coast until Ranch came along, but persistent rumors regarding the origin of its name really need to be addressed. I regret to inform all you Trekkies out there that it was not named after the green dancing girl from Orion, and connoisseurs of the silver screen will be disappointed to learn it was also not named for the foliage-wearing priestess in that timeless cinema classic *Love Slaves of the Amazon*. It was actually created in 1923 by the Executive Chef of San Francisco's Palace Hotel to honor hotel guest George Arliss, who at the time was appearing in the hit play *The Green Goddess*. It is still the hotel's signature dressing.

Wha' Cha' Need:

Electric Mixer or Blender

One clove of garlic
Two cups of mayonnaise
Four anchovy filets, minced
One green onion, chopped
Two teaspoons of chopped parsley
Two teaspoons of chopped chives
Two tablespoons of tarragon vinegar (or to taste)
One teaspoon of dried or cut fresh, tarragon
Salt and pepper to taste

Wha' Cha' Do:

Mix all of the ingredients together thoroughly, but do not puree completely. This should not be a completely smooth dressing. Serve it over mixed greens, (Dungeness) crab, steamed artichokes, or broiled fish. Makes about four servings.

GREEK SALAD (TARPON SPRINGS, FL)

Most people are unaware that the second part of the saying, "Beware of Greeks bearing gifts" is, "… unless they are bearing a salad!" Tarpon Springs is known as the *Natural Sponge Capital of the World*, and the sponge diving boats that ply its offshore waters are often owned by the families of Greek immigrants who first came to the area back in 1905. This recipe comes from the famous *Louis Pappas Restaurant* that has been in business since 1925. It is worth the effort to make this unusual salad, which can be served as either a main course or a side dish. After only few bites, you will shout "Opa!" and begin throwing plates.

Wha' Cha' Need:

Cooking pot
Glass mixing bowls
Large Serving platter

The Potato Salad:
Six medium-sized boiling potatoes
One to two tablespoons of red wine vinegar
Salt to taste
Four whole green onions, finely chopped
¼ cup of fresh parsley, finely chopped
½ cup of whole green onions thinly sliced
½ cup of mayonnaise

The Green Salad:
One medium-sized head of iceberg lettuce
12 roka (Greek vegetable) leaves, or 12 sprigs of watercress
Two ripe tomatoes, each of them cut into six wedges
One medium-sized cucumber, peeled and cut lengthwise into eight fingers
One medium-sized avocado, also peeled and cut into wedges
The juice from ½ of a lemon
Four (three-inch square portions) of feta cheese
One green bell pepper, cut into eight rings

Four canned beet slices
Four large shrimp, cooked and peeled
Four anchovy filets
12 Greek (Kalamata) olives
12 Greek (Salonika) peppers
Four to eight radishes, cut into flowers
Three to eight whole green onions
½ cup of distilled white vinegar
½ cup of olive oil
Oregano to taste

Wha' Cha' Do:

The Potato Salad:
Cook the unpeeled potatoes in unsalted water until they are tender (roughly 20 minutes) then let them cool until you can handle them. Peel the potatoes, cut them into bite-sized chunks, and place them into a large bowl. Sprinkle them with the red wine vinegar and salt, and add the finely chopped green onions. In another bowl, combine the chopped parsley, sliced green onions, mayonnaise, and salt, then add this to the potato chunks and mix it all together well.

The Green Salad:
Line a large platter with outer lettuce leaves and mound the potato salad in the center. Shred the rest of the lettuce, place it on top of the potato salad, and top it with the roka leaves (or watercress sprigs). Place the tomato wedges around the outer edge, alternating them with the cucumber slices. Sprinkle the avocado wedges with lemon juice, then add them. Arrange the feta cheese squares, green pepper rings, beet slices, shrimp, and anchovy filets on top, and place the olives, Salonika peppers, radish flowers, and whole green onions around the edge. Just before serving, sprinkle the salad with the distilled white vinegar, then olive oil, and finally the oregano. Makes about four main dish servings.

MAYFAIR DRESSING (ST. LOUIS, MO)

When I was just a wee Buckerino, my family would occasionally mosey down the mighty Mississippi to St. Louis and stay at the old *Mayfair Hotel*. Besides having guests like Cary Grant, Irving Berlin, and Harry Truman; the Mayfair was famous for a bell captain that somehow remembered everyone's name, and a very unique salad dressing. The Mayfair Hotel is just a memory these days, but here is the recipe for their signature dressing:

Wha' Cha' Need:

Pepper grinder
Blender

One tablespoon of whole black peppercorns
Two cloves of fresh garlic
½ of a sweet white onion
Three stalks of fresh celery
Eight ounces of canola or corn oil
One tablespoon of prepared mustard
Three whole eggs
Two ounces of anchovy paste
½ cup of champagne

Wha' Cha' Do:

Coarsely grind the peppercorns. Combine with all of the remaining ingredients in a blender and mix thoroughly. Serve over green salad. Makes about one quart.

MILLIONAIRE'S SALAD (NEWPORT, RI)

As Mrs. Thurston Spinnaker-Van der Snoot III once remarked while chatting around the punchbowl during a springtime gala at *The Breakers*, "If you need to ask how much this recipe costs to make dahling, you probably cannot afford it!"

Wha' Cha' Need:

Large cooking pot(s)
Glass mixing bowl
Saucepan

The Meat:
One medium live lobster
One bay leaf
One sprig of thyme

The Veggies:
One and ½ pounds of new potatoes, scrubbed
Two ripe tomatoes
Four oranges

The Dressing:
Two tablespoons of orange juice concentrate
Six tablespoons of unsalted butter, diced
Cayenne pepper
Salt

The Greens:
½ head of chicory or radicchio
One head of Boston lettuce
¼ cup of extra virgin olive oil
One (7 ounce) can of young artichokes in brine, quartered
One small bunch of tarragon, chervil or flat leaf parsley to garnish

Wha' Cha' Do:

The Meat:
Cook the lobster in a pot of salted water with the bay leaf and thyme. Bring the water to a boil and simmer for 15 minutes. Cool the lobster under running water. Remove the meat from the legs, claws, and tail, slice it into bite sized chunks, and set them aside.

The Veggies:
Bring the potatoes to a boil in salted water and simmer for 20 minutes. Drain, cover and keep warm. Cover the tomatoes with boiling water for 20 seconds to loosen their skins. Cool under running water and slip off the skins. Halve the tomatoes, discard the seeds, and coarsely dice the flesh. Peel and segment the oranges, over a small bowl. Set aside.

The Dressing:
Measure the thawed orange juice concentrate into a glass bowl and set it over a pan containing one inch of simmering water. Heat the juice concentrate for one minute, remove it from the heat then whisk in a little butter at a time until the dressing reaches a coating consistency. Season it to taste with the cayenne pepper and salt, cover, and keep the dressing warm.

The Greens:
Wash the salad greens and spin dry. Dress with olive oil, and divide into four servings. Moisten the potatoes, artichokes, and orange segments with olive oil and scatter them among the salad greens. Place the sliced lobster on top, and spoon on the warm dressing. Add the diced tomato and garnish with sprigs of fresh tarragon. Serve at room temperature. Serves four … and Ta-Ta my dear!

RUMMY FRUIT SALAD (JAMAICA)

Sugar plantation workers discovered that molasses could be fermented, and the rest is history. Some maintain that the name of the resulting liquor was derived from *roemers*, the word for large drinking glasses used by Dutch mariners who were called *rummers*. Others claim that the name came from *rumbullion*, which means "a great uproar." In Spain it is called *ron* and in France it is *rhum*, but it is also known as Nelson's Blood, Demon Water, and Kill-Devil. Early Caribbean rums were dark, heavy, and were not known for being of very high quality until Don Bacardi Masso began making the type of light rum used in this recipe which combines two major ingredients of Caribbean cuisine … tropical fruit and rum.

Wha' Cha' Need:

Glass mixing bowl

One star fruit, sliced
One cup of fresh pineapple chunks
Two oranges, peeled and sectioned
Two mangoes, peeled and cut into cubes
Two bananas, peeled and sliced into rounds
¼ cup of light Caribbean rum
½ cup of grated coconut, toasted

Wha' Cha' Do:

Mix all of the fruit, except for the toasted coconut, together in a glass bowl. Pour the rum over the fruit, and mix it well. Allow the fruit salad to stand for at least 30 minutes. Just before serving, sprinkle it with the toasted coconut. If some of your fruit is not quite ripe, you can sweeten to taste with raw sugar or honey. Serves four to six Rummies.

Note—If you absolutely must serve this to a bunch of very small children or lily-livered landlubbers, you could substitute whipped topping for the rum. Arrrh!

THOUSAND ISLAND DRESSING (CLAYTON, NY)

It may surprise you to learn that this popular dressing has a nautical origin. In the early days of the 20th century, there was a local guide named George Lalonde Jr. in the small resort village of Clayton in upstate New York. He took his clients on fishing trips in the Thousand Islands region near Lake Ontario and the Saint Lawrence Seaway. George and his wife Sophia also served them "shore dinners," including salads with a unique dressing. One such client was a prominent stage actress named May Irwin. May got the dressing recipe from Sophia, christened it "Thousand Island," and passed it on to the owner of the Waldorf Astoria hotel in New York City who made it famous. Besides being quite popular, it is still the only salad dressing that is named after a geographical area of the United States.

Wha' Cha' Need:

Glass mixing bowl

One cup of mayonnaise
¼ cup of commercial Chili Sauce
1/8 cup of pimiento-stuffed green olives, finely chopped
Two tablespoons of fresh green bell pepper, finely chopped
One hard-boiled egg, peeled and finely chopped
One scallion, finely chopped
A dash of Tabasco (optional)

Wha' Cha' Do:

Blend all of the above ingredients together. Cover and refrigerate it for at least an hour before serving. Serve over salad greens. Makes about two cups of dressing.

VILLAGE PILLAGE

Folks are surprised to learn that a number of early vessels carried poultry and other livestock on board as sources of meat, eggs, milk, and more intelligent conversation. As devout opportunists, buccaneers and pirates seldom passed up a chance to "liberate" animals from captured vessels or to put ashore to "borrow" chickens, pigs, ducks, cows, and geese from farms and other settlements. When such purloined food items were seasoned with similarly purloined spices, they provided these scallywags with a more varied and healthier diet than that of many honest seamen. Here are some land-based recipes for you.

AKOHO SY VOANIO (MADAGASCAR)

With its sheltered coves and proximity to Indian Ocean trade routes, Madagascar is known for being home to some of the world's fiercest pirates. This traditional recipe has been around ever since King Andrianampoinimerina (wow!) united all of the various tribes then said, "Vizako aho, noana aho," which as you all know means "I'm tired and I'm hungry!" (Recipe courtesy of King what's-his-name)

Wha' Cha' Need:

Clean cloth
Large sauté pan

One chicken, cut up
Two tomatoes
One fresh coconut
Two onions
Two garlic cloves
Four teaspoons of ginger
Oil, salt, and pepper

Wha' Cha' Do:

Sprinkle the chicken pieces with salt and pepper to taste. Slice the tomatoes into small cubes, and set aside. Shred the coconut meat into a clean cloth, and fold it around the shredded coconut meat. Wct the cloth with warm water, squeeze it to extract the coconut milk, and discard the shredded coconut meat. OK, if a fresh coconut is not available, you may also substitute a can of unsweetened coconut milk. Add a small amount of oil to a pan. Sauté the chicken pieces over medium heat until done then add the onions to the pan. Continue stirring over medium heat until the onions are brown. Add the ginger, tomatoes, and garlic to the pan. Sauté together briefly over medium heat, and add the coconut milk. Mix it well, reduce the heat, and simmer it over low heat for 30 more minutes. Serves four.

BOILED DINNER (NEW ENGLAND)

For over two hundred years most of the food eaten by New Englanders was boiled in heavy iron pots and served in large communal bowls. Forks were rarely found aboard most ships, so crewmembers cut larger chunks up into smaller ones with knives and primarily ate with their hands. This traditional dish proves that some things, including New Englanders' table manners, never change. Often served as a hearty mid-day meal, this dish was begun shortly after breakfast, simmered for hours, and it required little attention while people attended to other tasks. It was simply called "Boiled Dinner" up until 1896, when the name "New England Boiled Dinner" was introduced. Whatever you call it, here is how you can make it.

Wha' Cha' Need:

Cooking pot
Serving platter

One (4 pound) corned beef roast
Four quarts of cold water
Five medium potatoes
Five large carrots
Three large onions
Two large turnips
One medium head of cabbage

Wha' Cha' Do:

Rinse the corned beef roast in cold water. Cover the roast with water, bring it to a boil, and drain. Discard this water, which will be very salty. Cover the meat again with four more quarts of water and let it simmer until tender (e.g., several hours). Remove the meat from the water, but reserve this broth (you should have at least three pints). Keep the meat warm while the vegetables are cooking.

Peel the potatoes, carrots, onions, and turnips, and cut them and the head of cabbage into quarters. Add the quartered onions to the broth and cook for 30 minutes, then add the rest of the quartered vegetables and cook it for 25 to 30 minutes longer or until the vegetables are tender. Remove the vegetables from the broth with a slotted spoon to prevent them from getting soggy. Serve on a large platter with the meat in the middle. Horseradish and tangy mustard are typical condiments, but some folks also like a sprinkling of cider vinegar.

CHICKEN ADOBO (THE PHILIPPINES)

Some preparation methods grew out of necessity, and cooking in vinegar is one way to preserve food and allow it to be stored for longer periods of time at room temperatures. Adobo or *adobong* is sometimes called that national dish of the Philippines, and this easy version of *Adobong Na Manok* (Chicken Adobo) only takes about an hour to make. The marinating is optional, you can experiment with the type of vinegar, and the soy sauce to vinegar ratio can be adjusted to your taste.

Wha' Cha' Need:

Large pot

4 to 5 pounds of chicken thighs
½ cup of white vinegar
½ cup of soy sauce
Four cloves of garlic, crushed
One teaspoon of freshly ground black pepper
Three bay leaves
Steamed rice

Wha' Cha' Do:

Combine all of the ingredients in a large pot. Cover and let it marinate for one to three-hours. Bring it to a boil then lower the heat. Cover it and let it simmer for 30 minutes, stirring occasionally. Next uncover and simmer for about 20 more minutes, until the sauce is reduced and thickened and the chicken is tender. Serve it with steamed rice. Serves six to eight.

COCONUT CHICKEN (SAMOA)

Due to lingering after-effects of extensive personal research into native drinking customs, I cannot recall from exactly where in Polynesia this recipe came. But after you taste it, you will probably insist that you want "samoa!" The Samoan islands lie about halfway between Hawaii and New Zealand in the South Pacific, and prior to the 20th century were called the Navigator's Islands. Coconut and cream are common ingredients in Samoan dishes, which typically are not highly seasoned.

Wha' Cha' Need:

Large skillet
Shallow baking dish

Two tablespoons of butter
Two pounds of chicken pieces
Two cups of celery, sliced diagonally into one-inch long pieces
One medium onion, chopped
½ teaspoon of ground ginger
One (10½ ounce) can of condensed cream of chicken soup, undiluted
One (11 ounce) can of mandarin oranges, drained
¼ cup of shredded coconut
Salt and pepper to taste

Wha' Cha' Do:

In a large skillet, melt the butter over medium low heat. Add the chicken and brown; add the celery pieces, onion, and ginger; and cook until the vegetables are tender. Remove the chicken and place it with the skin side down into a shallow baking dish. Add the soup to the skillet; stir to loosen any brown bits then pour it over chicken. Bake the casserole at 375 degrees F for 30 minutes. Turn the chicken over; and bake it for 30 more minutes. Top it with the mandarin orange slices and the shredded coconut during the last ten minutes of baking. Salt and pepper it to taste. Serves four.

CREAMED CHICKEN (GEORGIA)

When y'all mosey down to the land of pecans and peaches, y'all had best be fixin' to enjoy some real southern eats. Folks here don't cater that much to tofu, but do like their butter. This here's a recipe that'll make y'all do the hambone and shout, "Good groceries!"

Wha' Cha' Need:

Large saucepan

Three tablespoons of butter
Eight ounces of fresh sliced mushrooms
Two tablespoons of finely chopped green bell pepper
Two tablespoons of finely chopped red bell pepper
¼ cup of chopped green onion
Four tablespoons of flour
One teaspoon of salt
1/8 teaspoon of ground pepper
One and ¾ cups of half-and-half
Two cups of chicken broth
Three cups of cooked diced chicken
Toast, pastry shells, or cooked rice

Wha' Cha' Do:

Melt the butter in a large saucepan. Add the mushrooms, green and red pepper, and green onion; cook for five minutes, until tender. Blend in the flour, salt, and pepper. Gradually add the half-and-half and chicken broth, stirring constantly. Continue cooking it over low to medium-low heat, stirring constantly, until the mixture is hot and thickened. Cook it for about one minute; add the chicken and heat it through. Serve it over toast, in pastry shells, or with rice. Serves eight.

CURRIED COCONUT GOAT (TRINDAD)

I once overheard a tourist in a local waterfront restaurant say, "Studies have shown that *calamari* is better for you than ordinary squid." I realize that you might not be as accustomed to eating goat as the folks in Trinidad, so if you do not like it you can try making this dish using *cabra*. It could be better for you.

Wha' Cha' Need:

Large heavy skillet

One and ½ pounds of goat (or lamb) meat
Two tablespoons of clarified butter or vegetable oil
One medium-sized onion, finely chopped
Two cloves of fresh garlic, minced
Three Yellow Wax hot peppers
One tablespoon of freshly grated ginger
Two teaspoons of ground coriander
One teaspoon of turmeric
½ teaspoon of freshly ground black pepper
Two teaspoons of powdered red chilies
One teaspoon of ground cumin
One and ½ cups of water
Two (or more) tablespoons of coconut cream
Salt to taste
Chutney

Wha' Cha' Do:

Cut the goat (cabra) or lamb meat up into ½ inch cubes. While the butter or oil is heating in a skillet, remove the stems, septa, and seeds from the Yellow Wax hot peppers and chop them up finely. Sauté the chopped onion, minced garlic, chopped peppers, and freshly grated ginger for roughly five minutes, stirring occasionally. Add the coriander, turmeric, black pepper, powdered chilies, and cumin, and sauté for another three minutes while stirring constantly. Add the meat to the skillet and brown it, stirring occasionally. Next add the water and simmer for about an hour (or until the meat chunks are tender), adding more water if the mixture gets too dry. Stir in the coconut cream, and cook for five more minutes. Add salt to your taste, and serve with chutney of your choice. Makes about four servings.

DRY RUB RIBS (MEMPHIS, TN)

Memphis is sometimes called "River City," and here is a recipe for you river rats from the place that is also known for being home to the blues, rockabilly, rock n' roll, and great pork barbeque. It uses a dry rub, which is the way some locals claim barbeque is meant to be. Whenever Elvis ate these ribs he would say, "Thank you, thank you very much!"

Wha' Cha' Need:

Shallow dish
Mixing bowl
Plastic wrap
Covered barbeque grill
Oak or Hickory Wood chips
Drip pan

Four pounds of meaty pork ribs
One tablespoon of brown sugar
One tablespoon of onion powder
¾ teaspoon of ground cumin
½ teaspoon of black pepper
One tablespoon of paprika
¾ teaspoon of celery salt
Water

Wha' Cha' Do:

Scrape the silver membrane from the under side of the ribs. Trim off the "flap" from the large end of the slab(s), and cook it as an additional portion. Cut the remaining ribs into four portions and place them into a shallow dish. Combine the brown sugar, onion powder, cumin, black pepper, paprika, and celery salt in a mixing bowl, and rub the mixture evenly over the meaty side of the ribs. Wrap them in plastic and marinate them in the refrigerator for 4 to 24 hours. Soak the wood chips in water for at least an hour before grilling, then drain. Place the charcoal around a drip pan inside a grill with a cover, and add about ½ inch of hot water to drip pan. Sprinkle half of the drained wood chips over the hot coals. Place the ribs, bone side down, on the grill rack over the drip pan. Cover and grill for 1½ to 2 hours or until the ribs are tender … adding more wood chips as needed. Serves four (or more).

FOUR HAPPINESS PORK (SHANGHAI, CHINA)

As anyone who has read *Captain Bucko's Nauti-Words Handbook* already knows, the term "Shanghaied" originated when it was very difficult to get crewmembers to sign on for long or arduous voyages. Men who had been drugged or knocked unconscious by creative ship owners and Masters sometimes found themselves aboard vessels bound for remote ports like Shanghai, and local authorities rid themselves of troublemakers by "shipping them to Shanghai." The following recipe is for a Shanghai specialty that is common in local households

Wha' Cha' Need:

Cooking pot(s) with lid

One and ½ pounds of lean pork
One cup of water
Two tablespoons of rice wine
Six tablespoons of soy sauce
Two slices of ginger
One scallion, chopped
Two tablespoons of sugar

Wha' Cha' Do:

Put the pork into a pot of boiling water, and simmer it for ten minutes. Drain and rinse it in cold water, then cut the pork into two-inch cubes. Put the pork cubes and one cup of water into a heavy cooking pot, and bring it to a boil. Add the wine, soy sauce, ginger, and scallion. Cover the pot tightly, and simmer it over very low heat for two hours. Add the sugar, increase the heat to high, and baste it until the gravy coats the meat. Serve it with rice, steamed buns, or vegetables. Serves four to six.

HULI HULI CHICKEN (KAILUA, HI)

Attending several old-fashioned Hawaiian house parties is an experience that I will never forget. There were usually *tutus* (grandmothers) playing their ukuleles, *kamainas* (natives) drinking Primo beer or a very strange concoction of milk and Crown Royale, men and women dancing hulas, and plenty of local food. Hawaii's own version of barbecued chicken is cooked with huli-huli sauce, which is made from brown sugar, soy sauce, fresh ginger, garlic, and other *ono* (tasty) stuff.

Wha' Cha' Need:

Oven or outdoor grill
Glass mixing bowl

Five pounds of chicken pieces
1/3 cup of ketchup
1/3 cup of soy sauce
½ cup of brown sugar
Three tablespoons of sherry
One piece of ginger root, crushed
One clove garlic, crushed

Wha' Cha' Do:

Arrange the chicken with the skin side up, on an oven broiler pan on an outdoor grill. Broil it six to eight inches from the broiler unit in an oven for ten minutes on each side or cook it on an outdoor grill. Combine the remaining ingredients and baste the chicken pieces. Continue broiling/grilling it for ten more minutes on each side, while basting it frequently with the sauce. *Shaka!*

JUMBUCK IN A TUCKERBAG (AUSTRALIA)

G'day, mates! The name for this particular dish comes from a line in the song *Waltzing Matilda*, and what could be more Australian than that? But before you even ask, it does not contain any kangaroo or iguana meat. No worries!

Wha' Cha' Need:

Food processor
Frying pan
Cake racks
Baking sheet

The Dish:
One-pound rack of lamb
¼ cup of chopped onion
½ teaspoon of dried mint leaves or two fresh mint leaves
½ teaspoon of dried, or one sprig of fresh rosemary
½ teaspoon of dried, or one sprig of fresh parsley
One whole egg
½ cup of breadcrumbs
½ teaspoon of Worcestershire sauce
Salt and pepper, to taste
Two tablespoons of vegetable oil
One package of frozen puff pastry dough, thawed

Pastry Wash:
One egg yolk
One tablespoon of milk

Wha' Cha' Do:

The Dish:
Trim the fat from the lamb and cut the meat into cubes. Chop them up with the onion and herbs in a food processor. Add the egg, breadcrumbs, Worcestershire sauce, salt, and pepper and mix together. Form the lamb

into four patties. Heat the oil in a frying pan and when it is hot, sear the patties on both sides but don't cook them through. Cool the patties on paper towels and allow them to stand in the refrigerator until they are cool to the touch. Roll out the thawed puff pastry dough to about 1/8 inch thick. Cut the puff pastry dough into four circles that are roughly eight inches in diameter each. Place a cleaned rack bone into top of each patty and place the patties in center of the puff pastry circles. Draw up the sides of the pastry circles around the bones. Cut a small slit into the top of each "bag" for steam to escape, tie the top of each bag with a piece of cooked spaghetti, and place the pastry bags onto lightly greased cake racks over a baking sheet.

The Pastry Wash:
Make an egg wash using one egg yolk and one tablespoon of milk. Brush this mixture onto the bags. Bake them in a 450 degree F oven for 10 to 15 minutes. Serves four mates or sheilas.

KAHLUA PORK TENDERLOINS (MEXICO)

The more perceptive among you may notice that the first word in this recipe is not spelled the same as the first word in the next recipe. That is because this dish is made with the Mexican coffee-flavored liqueur named Kahlua, whereas the next recipe uses the ancient Hawaiian term for "a big ugly pig cooked in a hole and fed to mainland tourists at luaus."

Wha' Cha' Need:

Saucepan
Shallow dish or re-sealable plastic bag
Covered baking dish or aluminum foil

½ cup of Kahlua liqueur
½ cup of butter or margarine
Two (¾ pound each) pork tenderloins
One teaspoon of lemon-pepper seasoning
½ teaspoon of garlic salt with parsley

Wha' Cha' Do:

Combine the Kahlua and butter in a small saucepan; and bring it to a boil. Boil it for four minutes, stirring often. Remove it from the heat, and let cool slightly. Slice the pork tenderloins crosswise about one and ½ inch thick, cutting to but not through the bottoms. Sprinkle the tenderloins with the lemon-pepper seasoning and garlic salt; and place them into a large shallow dish or a large heavy-duty plastic bag. Pour half of the Kahlua mixture over the pork tenderloins. Cover the dish or seal the bag securely, and marinate the meat in the refrigerator for four hours, turning occasionally. Also cover and refrigerate the remaining Kahlua mixture. Remove the tenderloins, and discard the marinade. Grill the meat while covered over medium to hot coals, or in a 350 to 400 degrees F oven until a meat thermometer inserted into the thickest portion of the tenderloins indicates 160 degrees F, turning once and basting occasionally with the rest of the Kahlua mixture. Cover and let them stand for ten minutes before slicing. Serves four.

KALUA PUA'A (LIHUE, HI)

Kauai is one of the oldest of the main Sandwich (Hawaiian) Islands, and locals there were roasting pork long before outsiders came there to film South Pacific, Blue Hawaii, or Fantasy Island. But if you are planning to have a luau in your neighborhood, you just might run into a few problems. The local supermarket could be out of whole pigs, *ti* leaves, or volcanic rocks; and your spouse may be somewhat reluctant to let you dig an *imu* (pit) in your front yard. What should you do? Try the following *haole* (foreigner) recipe!

Wha' Cha' Need:

Glass mixing bowl
Roasting pan with cover
Two large forks to shred

One tablespoon of rock salt
¾ teaspoon of minced garlic
Three tablespoons of low salt soy sauce
One tablespoon of fresh ginger, grated
Three to four pound pork roast, slashed

Wha' Cha' Do:

Combine all of the above ingredients and rub the mixture over the pork roast. Place it into a roasting pan or a clay roaster. Cover and roast the pork for four hours at 325 degrees F. Use two forks to shred the meat, and serve while hot.

L.A. BREAKFAST PIE (FAIRHOPE, AL)

An old Navy buddy used to claim his family came from L.A. (i.e., Lower Alabama), and you cannot get much farther south in that state than Mobile without getting a little bit wet. This recipe for L.A. Breakfast Pie comes from the shore of Mobile Bay, and this dish might help the morning after you have indulged in just a few too many of those infamous *'Bama Slammers*. Recipe courtesy of the Bay Breeze Bed and Breakfast.

Wha' Cha' Need:

Nine-inch pie plate
Mixing bowl

De Crust:
Three cups of shredded taters
Five tablespoons of melted buttah

De Fillin':
One cup of finely chopped cooked ham
½ cup of finely chopped onion
½ cup of chopped green pepper
¼ cup of drained and diced pimento
One packed cup of shredded sharp cheese
Three medium-size eggs
½ cup of whole milk
½ teaspoon of salt
Pepper to taste

Wha' Cha' Do:

De Crust:
Pat the shredded taters with paper towels to remove any excess moisture then press them onto the bottom and the sides of a nine-inch pie plate that has been drizzled with buttah. Bake it at 425 degrees F for about 25 to 35 minutes or until it is golden brown then let the crust cool on a wire rack.

De Fillin':

After the baked crust has cooled, layer in the chopped cooked ham, onion, green pepper, pimento, and shredded cheese. Mix the eggs, milk, salt, and pepper up together in a separate bowl then pour this mixture over the top of all the other ingredients. Bake at 375 degrees F for 35 to 40 minutes or until set, and let it stand for ten minutes before serving. Serves four.

LEATHER SATCHELS (DESPARATE DINING)

Things could get a little dicey when the food became scarce on some pirate ships. After Charlotte de Berry's crew ran out of victuals they reportedly ate two slaves and her husband, which in turn saved her quite a bundle in divorce lawyer fees. In 1670, Sir Henry Morgan's crew resorted to eating their leather satchels. Just in case you ever find yourself in a similar situation, here is their actual recipe courtesy of Sir Henry himself.

Wha' Cha' Need:

Water
A rock
A scraper
A sharp knife
A leather satchel

Wha' Cha' Do:

Cut the leather satchel up into strips. Tenderize by soaking them in water, and pounding them with rocks (ballast stones work well). Scrape off any hair, then roast or grill the strips prior to cutting them into bite-sized tidbits. Serve with lots of water. This recipe makes enough for one to four privateers, depending upon their current degree of starvation.

PAPEETE PORK CHOPS (TAHITI)

As you all probably know, when Fletcher Christian and his fellow mutineers from the *HMS Bounty* returned to Tahiti (then called Otaheite) in 1789, it was because during an earlier visit they had become fascinated with how the Tahitian women wiggled their pork chops in time with pulsating native rhythms. This time-tested recipe is quite popular with everyone except the pigs in Tahiti. And just in case you don't have an *ahimaa* (pit) in your yard, you can even cook it in your oven.

Wha' Cha' Need:

Skillet
Baking dish
Blender

Eight pork chops
¾ cup of cooking sherry
1/3 cup of soy sauce
¼ cup of salad oil
One clove of garlic
One teaspoon of ground ginger
1/3 teaspoon of oregano
One tablespoon of maple syrup
Salt and pepper to taste

Wha' Cha' Do:

Pre-heat your oven (or ahimaa) to 350 degrees F. While doing this, brown the pork chops in a skillet then transfer them to a baking dish. Put all of the other ingredients into a blender and process until smooth. Pour the mixture over the pork chops, cover, and bake them for 1 to 1½ hours until they are tender, turning once during this time to brown both sides. Serves eight mutineers.

PULLUM FRONTONIANUM (ANCIENT ROME)

After ol' Marcus Gavius Apicius worked up an appetite watching his galley slaves row him about the Mediterranean, he would have some of them prepare him this tasty chicken dish. The original recipe called for some unfamiliar ingredients like *liquamen,* *saturei,* and *defritum.* But if you do not currently have any of these in your pantry fear not, for I have provided you with worthy substitutes in the following recipe.

About Liquamen:
Also sometimes called *garum,* the Ancient Romans made this sauce by fermenting fatty fish in brine with other flavorings. You could try using Asian fish sauces, or just substitute a little red wine and salt as in this recipe.

About Saturei::
This is a flowering plant that commonly grows in Southern Europe. It was used as a spice. This recipe substitutes dried rose petals. So who's gonna know?

About Defritum:
This thick syrup could probably be made by reducing fig juice, but this recipe takes the easy way out by using the syrup from a can of figs.

Wha' Cha' Need:

Mixing bowl
Large frying pan
Large baking dish
Large serving platter

Spice Mixture:
One cup of red wine
One teaspoon of salt
½ cup of olive oil
One leek bulb, chopped
¼ cup of fresh dill, chopped

1/3 cup of dried rose petals, chopped
Two tablespoons of ground coriander seed
½ teaspoon of ground black pepper

The Pullum:
Two tablespoons of olive oil
One (three pound) whole chicken
½ cup of syrup from canned figs
Salt and pepper to taste

Wha' Cha' Do:

Spice Mixture:
Combine the red wine, teaspoon of salt, ½ cup of olive oil, chopped leek bulb and chopped dill weed, dried rose petals, ground coriander and pepper in a bowl.

The Pullum::
Heat two tablespoons of olive oil in a large frying pan. Fry the whole chicken over medium heat, add about half of the above spice mixture to the pan, and continue to cook until the chicken just begins to change color. Place the whole chicken into a baking dish along with all of the spice mixture, and rub the bird with the spice mixture for a minute or so. Bake it at 425 degrees F for about one hour, basting occasionally with the spice mixture. The chicken will almost appear burnt when it is done. Place the chicken onto a serving platter that has been moistened with fig syrup, and season with salt and pepper to taste. Serves four friends, Romans, or countrymen.

STUFFED HEN (PIRATE RECIPE)

You should note that this traditional pirate recipe does not specify any particular type of bird, which typically concerns many members of the Audubon Society. One of the most interesting things about this recipe is its requirement to sew up any holes. So if you tend to be a little overzealous with your musket or cutlass, you might want to consider blud-  geoning ... and do not be concerned if your hen looks like it has a serious skin disorder.

Wha' Cha' Need:

Mixing bowl
Needle & thread

¼ pound of butter
One teaspoon of sugar
One teaspoon of cinnamon
One and ½ cups of currants
One large hen (of some sort)

Wha' Cha' Do:

If your bird is not already bald, pluck it. Mix the currants, sugar, cinnamon, and butter together, and stuff the mixture into your hen. After you sew up any holes, press the stuffing out beneath the skin all around the bird. Put it into a suitable container and cook it in a 300 degree F oven until it is done. Using your knives and your bare hands, devour it handily while making obnoxious sounds.

WALKABOUT STEAK (AUSTRALIA)

Devotees of classical music realize that "Walkabout" is the title of a song by the *Red Hot Chile Peppers*, and in England it means an organized event during which members of the Royal Family stroll past assembled onlookers to meet and to chat with members of the public. Down under however, it is a (quasi)pidgin term that refers to the belief that at about the age of thirteen Aborigines "go walkabout" in the outback for six months as a rite of passage. If you happen to be embarking upon such a journey, you may want to fortify yourself with one last decent meal.

Wha' Cha' Need, Mate:

Ovenproof dish
Glass mixing bowl

Two pounds of sirloin steak
Two onions, finely chopped
Two teaspoons of brown sugar
Two teaspoons of salt
½ teaspoon of ground black pepper
A pinch of ground cayenne pepper
Two teaspoons of capers, chopped
Two teaspoons of mixed herbs, including thyme, sage, and oregano
1/3 cup of ketchup
Two teaspoons of Worcestershire sauce
1/3 cup of vinegar

Wha' Cha' Do:

You can adjust the ingredients of this dish to your taste (e.g., some mates prefer to reduce the amount of vinegar). Trim the steak and cut it into pieces. Place it into an ovenproof dish and cover it with the chopped onions. Mix all of the other ingredients together, and pour the mixture over the top of the meat and onions. Cover and refrigerate for at least two hours. Bake while covered with aluminum foil or an ovenproof lid, at 350 degrees F for about 50 to 60 minutes. Serves four.

Note—If this dish gets overcooked, you can always make hiking boots out of it.

YANKEE POT ROAST (NEW ENGLAND)

This dish evolved from the boiled dinner, except that the ingredients in this case are roasted in a covered pot instead of cooked in a kettle. That explains the "Pot Roast," but where did it get the rest of its name? The origin of the term "Yankee" has been the subject of debate. Some claim that it was derived from "Jan Kaas" (John Cheese), a derogatory nickname given to the Dutch by the Germans and Flemish in the 1600s. Others insist that it came from "Janke" (Little John), the nickname originally used for Dutch pirates and later for Dutch settlers along the Hudson River. During the Revolutionary War the British used the term "Yankee" for all Americans, but more specifically for New Englanders who were known for being ~~cheap~~ thrifty. These folks discovered that by first browning then cooking their meat slowly in covered pots with some vegetables, they could use cheaper cuts or even meat from their (former) working livestock. Yankee Pot Roast was created for economic reasons, and its name sounds better than "Frugal Stew!"

Wha' Cha' Need:

Large heavy pot with lid
Large serving platter

Vegetable cooking oil, (e.g., Canola)
Sea/kosher salt and freshly ground pepper
One bone-in (four to five pound) chuck roast
One large carrot, chopped
One stalk of celery, chopped
One medium onion, chopped
Four to five cloves of garlic, chopped
Three tablespoons of flour
Three and ½ cups of water
Two tablespoons of tomato paste
Two teaspoons of dried (or six sprigs of fresh) thyme
Two bay leaves
Eight to ten small onions
Five carrots cut into 1 to 2-inch long pieces

One pound of red potatoes (or white potatoes cut up)
One pound of large mushrooms, quartered

Wha' Cha' Do:

Pour in enough oil to cover the bottom of a large heavy pot over high heat. Trim excess fat off of the chuck roast, generously salt and pepper both sides, and sear the meat until it is well browned on both sides. Remove the roast, and pour off the oil. Return the pot to medium heat and add the chopped carrot, celery, onion and garlic. Cook while stirring, adding a small amount of oil if necessary, until the vegetables are softened but not browned. Sprinkle flour over the vegetables and stir for two to three more minutes. Return the meat to the pot, adding water, tomato paste, thyme, and bay leaves. Bring it to a simmer, cover (use aluminum foil under lid if it does not fit tightly). Place into preheated 325 degree F oven and cook for two hours. Check at one hour, turn meat if it is not covered by liquid, and add more water if the liquid gets too thick. It should be the consistency of thin gravy. At about 2 to 2¼ hours, add the remaining vegetables, and continue cooking for a total of 3 hours. If the vegetables are still not quite done, remove from the heat, and let it stand covered awhile. Add salt or pepper to taste. Skim the excess fat off the liquid, cut the meat into serving size pieces, arrange on a heated platter surrounded with vegetables, and moisten with some of the liquid. Serves about six hungry, yet thrifty, Yankees.

Note—There really is no single recipe for Yankee Pot Roast, and the vegetables included often depend upon what is available and less expensive at the time.

NETTABLE EDIBLES

Archeological evidence tells us that most ancient vessels operated in the vicinity of water, so seafood was often more readily available than say, mountain goats. Sailors fished during calmer weather, and gathered shellfish and other edibles in the shallows. Oceans, lakes, rivers, and other bodies of water provided what seemed to be an unlimited source of food, and a number of fascinating (and quite tasty) regional and local recipes evolved. This Chapter contains many of them.

ALDER PLANK SALMON (THE PACIFIC NORTHWEST)

This smoked salmon derives its flavor from alder wood planks. If you get these at a lumberyard, be sure you tell them that you are cooking on the planks so that you do not get any creosote or other treated wood. Make sure you know what size plank will fit into your smoker ... and do not get "board" while waiting!

Wha' Cha' Need:

Alder wood plank
Two mixing bowls
Glass baking dish
Basting brush
Smoker

The Brine:
This is a relatively basic brine mixture. You can also add white wine, soy sauce, and other herbs and spices as you like. This recipe will yield about one quart.

¼ cup of kosher salt
¼ cup of packed brown sugar
Four cups of water

The Fish Dish:
One (3 pound) fresh salmon filet
Freshly ground black pepper to taste
1/8 cup of packed brown sugar
One tablespoon of water

Wha' Cha' Do:

Make the brine by vigorously whisking the salt, brown sugar, and water together in a medium-sized bowl until all the salt and sugar is dissolved. Pour the brine mixture over the fish in a glass baking dish, ensuring that the meat is completely submerged. Soak the fish filet in the brine mixture for at least four hours, but preferably overnight. While doing this, submerge the alder wood plank in water, placing a heavy object on top of it to keep it from floating. Preheat the smoker to 160 to 180 degrees F. Remove the filet from the brine, rinse it thoroughly under cold running water, and pat it dry. Remove the plank from the water, and lay the fish out on it. Season the salmon filet (not the plank) with freshly ground black pepper. Smoke the fish for at least two hours, checking it after one and one-half hour for done-ness. Smoking fish can take between two and six hours depending upon your taste, the size of the filet, and the fat content of the fish. The salmon is done when it flakes with a fork, but it should not be too salty. As fish smokes, its salt content deceases. During the last 30 minutes of smoking, combine the brown sugar and water into a paste, and liberally brush this mixture onto the fish before serving. The smoked salmon serves roughly ten people, while the plank serves even more epicurious termites.

ALLIGATOR ETOUFFEE (CAJUN COUNTRY)

When gathering the ingredients for this dish, it may help to bear in mind that faster alligators just might be able to outrun slower humans. It is also a well-known fact that male alligators will bellow loudly when they hear a B-flat, but this may not be all that useful unless you happen to be a musician lost in the swamp. Alligator meat also contains fewer calories and less cholesterol than beef, pork, lamb, or chicken; but Cajuns compensate for this by including lots of butter in recipes like this one.

Wha' Cha' Need:

Sauté pan
Covered iron pot

Two medium-sized onions, chopped
Two cloves of fresh garlic, chopped
Four stalks of fresh celery, chopped
One bell pepper, chopped (optional)
Two sticks (½-pound) of butter
One can of Rotel brand tomatoes
One pound of gator, cut into thin strips
½ cup of green onion tops, chopped
¼ cup of fresh parsley, chopped
Salt and black pepper, to taste
Cayenne pepper, to taste
Cooked rice and French bread

Wha' Cha' Do:

Sauté da chopped onions, garlic, celery, (and optional bell pepper) in da butter 'til they be soft. Add da tomatoes and simmer for twenty minutes in yo' covered iron pot. Add da gator strips and cook over a low heat until tender ('bout an hour). If da gravy thickens too much while it's cookin', add some water. Add da chopped green onion tops and parsley during da last ten minutes of cookin', and season it to taste with da salt, black pepper, and cayenne. Serve over rice, with a slice of French bread for moppin' da plate. Serves four. *Aiiiyeee!*

CLAMBAKE (NEW ENGLAND)

When the Pilgrims arrived, they supposedly found Native Americans cooking soft-shelled clams by steaming them over hot rocks covered with seaweed. Although some New Englanders might not always know when or when not to pronounce the letter "r," they are proud of their clambakes. But, a more descriptive name for this famous regional dish would be "seafood, veggie, and seaweed parfait."

Wha' Cha' Need:

Sandy beach
Large stones
Dry firewood
Four cinder blocks
A metal grate/plate
A bunch of seaweed

Eight ears of corn
Eight purple potatoes
Eight fresh, live lobsters
Two kielbasa, split and cut into eight pieces each
Eight dozen hard shell (e.g., cherrystone, littleneck) clams
Two whole flounders, wrapped in aluminum foil with thyme, oil, and lemon slices
Eight dozen fresh, live oysters
A large tarp or pieces of burlap

Wha' Cha' Do:

Dig a shallow pit in the sand (or in your neighbor's yard) and line it with large stones. Gather driftwood and pile it on top of the stones. Create a bonfire by burning the wood for one to two hours until the stones are red hot. Rake off the ashes. Place a cinder block on each corner of the pit to form the base. Lay a grate (or piece of steel) on top to make a table. Gather seaweed and place a thick layer on the metal. Place the corn and the potatoes on the pile, and cover with a thin layer of seaweed. Mound the lobster tails, claws and kielbasa evenly on top, then cover with another thin layer of seaweed. Set the clams and the flounders on top and cover with another layer of seaweed. Finally, place the oysters on top, and cover with a thick layer of seaweed. The juice from the seafood will drip down and flavor the corn and potatoes. Cover the entire bake with burlap or a tarp soaked in seawater to trap in the seaweed steam and bake the food. Keep the tarp wet by pouring seawater over the top if needed. Cook until the clams open up and the lobster turns bright red, about 1 to 1½ hours. Serves eight.

COCONUT VANILLA PRAWNS (TAHITI)

If you can't make it to the next *tamaaraa* (Tahitian feast) in your neighborhood, this recipe will help make a regular *amura'a* (meal) feel like you are on Moorea. Tahitians are very proud of their vanilla, which is some of the best in the world. This recipe incorporates several tastes of the islands, but it is rather rich. You could use light coconut milk and/or substitute evaporated milk for the double cream if you want to lighten it a bit. Recipe courtesy of The Vanilla Queen.

Wha' Cha' Need:

Large frying pan

Two tablespoons of olive oil
Two pounds of raw prawns, peeled and de-veined
Four fluid ounces of dark rum
One vanilla bean, split lengthwise
Eight ounces of double cream
Six ounces of coconut milk
Salt and pepper to taste
Boiled rice

Wha' Cha' Do:

Heat the olive oil in a frying pan, add the prawns, and stir-fry for three minutes or until they turn pink. Remove the prawns from the pan, set them aside, and wipe the pan clean with a paper towel. Add the rum and the split vanilla bean pod to the pan, bring that mixture to a boil, and reduce it down to about two tablespoons. Next stir in the double cream and the coconut milk, and again reduce the resulting mixture by half. Scrape the seeds from the vanilla bean pod into the cream mixture and discard the vanilla bean pod. Season the sauce with salt and pepper, return the prawns to the pan, and cook it for one minute more stirring gently. Serve it immediately over boiled rice.

CRAWFISH MONICA (NATCHITOCHES, LA)

Folks in southern Louisiana claim that you just might be a "Closet Cajun" if: (1) watching *Wild Kingdom* makes you real hungry; and (2) you think that a lobster is just a crawfish on steroids. Here's one of the most popular dishes at the *New Orleans Jazz and Heritage Festival* every year, and if you do not have crawfish you can substitute shrimp, crab, or oysters. (Recipe courtesy of some Cajun named Monica)

Wha' Cha' Need:

Two large cooking pots

One stick (¼ pound) of real butter
Three to ten cloves of garlic, chopped
Two medium-sized onions, chopped
One pound of crawfish tails, boiled and peeled
One pint of whole (not skim) half-and-half
One to two tablespoons of Creole seasoning
One pound of cooked Rotelli pasta

Wha' Cha' Do:

Melt the butter in a large pot and sauté the chopped garlic and onions for three minutes. Add the crawfish tail meat and sauté for two more minutes. Stir in the half-and-half then add several generous pinches of the Creole seasoning, tasting in between pinches until you think it tastes right. Cook it for five to ten minutes more over medium heat until the sauce thickens.

Cook the pasta according to the directions on the package. Drain and rinse it under cool water, then repeat. Combine with the above mixture and toss well. Let it stand for ten minutes or so over very low heat, stirring often. Serve with hot French bread. Makes four to six servings.

FRIED BUFFALO (QUINCY, IL)

Before you go out shopping for a bison-sized deep fryer, you should know that the buffalo in this recipe refers to a large fish found in rivers and lakes. By the middle of the 19th century, the riverfront of my hometown was a bustling place. Within walking distance along Front Street, there was the Pacific House Hotel, the Kreitz Ice Company, Clat Adams' General Store, several restaurants, and ol' Patrick Tooley's Saloon that catered to the needs of those who traveled and worked the mighty Mississippi. *The River House* has been a landmark for many years, and is famous for their fried fish dinners. Here is one of their recipes, thanks to Sabina and Jim.

Wha' Cha' Need:

Shallow pan
Deep fryer

The Breading:
One cup of cornmeal
½ cup of flour
One teaspoon of lemon-pepper seasoning
½ teaspoon of garlic salt

The Fish Dish:
¾ pound of buffalo filets
Cooking Oil

Wha' Cha' Do:

Combine all of the breading ingredients in a shallow pan and mix together well. Score the fish filets every ¼ inch, and remove as many bones as possible. Open the scoring slits and pour the breading over the filets to coat them thoroughly. Shake off the excess breading, and fry the filets in 350 degree F oil for roughly 2½ minutes. Drain well, and serve them while hot.

GRILLED SAND DABS (MONTEREY, CA)

Monterey is known for its: spectacular scenery, Cannery Row, legendary golf courses with equally legendary green fees, music festivals, and sand dabs. The latter are small bottom-dwelling flatfish that are found as far north as Oregon, although "grilled dabs" have become one of Monterey's signature dishes. Purists sometimes eat them whole, but many prefer filets to avoid their tiny bones. Sand dabs might be small, but as that old saying goes, "a little dab'll do ya!"

Wha' Cha' Need:

Mixing bowl
Non-stick skillet

¼ cup of milk
One egg, beaten
One pound of sand dab filets
One cup of flour seasoned with salt and pepper
¼ cup of olive oil or clarified butter
Some baby greens
Lemon wedges

Wha' Cha' Do:

Beat the milk and egg together in a bowl. Dredge each filet in the seasoned flour, dip it into the egg/milk mixture, and roll it in the seasoned flour again until it is thoroughly coated. Heat the olive oil or clarified butter in a skillet over medium to high heat until it is hot. Gently place the filets into the skillet, and cook them for three to four minutes on each side until nicely golden brown on both, turning only once. Take them from the skillet and place them on paper towels to remove any excess oil. Serve them immediately on beds of baby greens, garnished with lemon wedges. Serves two.

Note—Sand dabs are so sweet they only need a squeeze of lemon, but you can also serve them with brown butter, beurre blanc, caper, or chermoula sauces.

JUST FOR THE HALIBUT (HOMER, AK)

Halibut are the largest of all flatfish and are some of the biggest fish in the ocean. Those that weigh more than 100 pounds are sometimes called "barn doors," and the largest ever caught while sport fishing in Alaska weighed 459 pounds. Prized for their delicate flavor, each halibut yields four large filets called *fletches*, plus even sweeter *cheeks* from its head area. Hardy Alaskans sometimes make this dish when they are entertaining wimps from the lower 48, but sometimes they fix it "just for the halibut."

Wha' Cha' Need:

Baking pan

Three pounds of halibut
Butter, salt, and pepper
Four strips of bacon
One cup of sour cream
One teaspoon of lemon Juice
1/3 cup of buttered breadcrumbs
½ cup of grated Parmesan cheese
Fresh parsley, finely chopped

Wha' Cha' Do:

Rub the halibut with butter, and salt and pepper to taste. Lay the bacon strips on the bottom of a baking pan, and place the halibut on top of the bacon. Mix the sour cream, the lemon juice, the breadcrumbs, and the grated Parmesan cheese together, and spread this mixture over the top of the halibut. Bake it at 350 degrees F until tender (about 20 to 30 minutes). Sprinkle it with more grated Parmesan cheese and finely chopped fresh parsley. Serves six.

OYSTERS ROCKEFELLER (NEW ORLEANS, LA)

Louisiana oysters are among the finest tasting in the whole world because of the things that are flushed down the Mississippi River. Legend tells us that this dish was created in 1899 by a New Orleans chef facing a shortage of European snails (a.k.a. escargot), and seeking a local substitute. He named the rich green sauce for his new dish after one of the richest men in America in those days, John D. Rockefeller. The original recipe remains a closely guarded secret at *Antoine's*, but here is one from an equally famous New Orleans restaurant.

Wha' Cha' Need:

Rock salt
Serving pie pans
Saucepan with cover
Pastry bag

One cup of chopped shallots
½ cup of chopped parsley
One and ½ cups of chopped spinach
½ cup of flour
One cup of melted butter
One cup of oyster liquor (juice)
Two cloves of garlic, minced
½ teaspoon of salt
¼ teaspoon of cayenne pepper
¼ cup of minced anchovy filets
Four ounces of Absinthe, Herbsaint, or Pernod
Three of four dozen fresh, live, oysters

Note—Finding the next to last ingredient in this recipe could be the most challenging, and most interesting. *Absinthe* (a.k.a. The Green Fairy) is a high-proof anise-flavored liquor that was quite popular in the late 19th and early 20th centuries, but was banned in the United States and many European countries by 1915 because it was said to be addictive. *Herbsaint* is the brand name of another anise-flavored liquor created in New Orleans in 1934, and first marketed under the name "Legendre Absinthe." *Pernod Fil* (pronounced pear´-no) is the oldest brand of absinthe, dating back to 1792 in Switzerland. Absinthe is currently undergoing a comeback in the European Union (EU). Selling absinthe remains illegal in the United States, but it is not illegal to possess or consume it.

Wha' Cha' Do:

Make a bed of rock salt in the bottoms of the serving pie pans for each serving, and place them into an oven to pre-heat the salt. Put the shallots, parsley, and spinach through a food chopper. In a saucepan, stir the flour into the melted butter, cook for five minutes, but do not let it brown. Blend in the oyster liquor (juice), garlic, salt, and cayenne pepper; then stir in the chopped greens and minced anchovy filets. Cover and simmer for 20 minutes. Add the Absinthe, Herbsaint, or Pernod, and cook uncovered until the mixture thickens. Open the oysters and place six of them per serving in the half shells onto the beds of rock salt. Put the sauce into a pastry bag, and pipe some of it onto each oyster. Bake them in a 400 degree F oven until the edges of the oysters start to curl (about five minutes for small oysters, and longer for large ones). Makes six to eight servings.

PAN-FRIED CATFISH (NATCHEZ, MS)

The oldest continuously inhabited settle-
ment on the Mississippi River; Natchez
became the first capital of the Mississippi
Territory in 1798. Perched high up on
the bluffs, *Upper Natchez* was known for
its antebellum mansions and before the
Civil War was home to more millionaires than any other state except New
York. *Lower Natchez* (also called "Under the Hill") developed along the
riverbank below the bluffs, and was a den of river pirates and prostitutes.
But some market needs change, and these days Mississippi farm-raised cat-
fish are also big business.

Wha' Cha' Need:

Two shallow dishes
Two large platters
Large frying pan

Four medium catfish filets, ¼ inch thick
One cup of cold milk
One cup of yellow cornmeal
Two or three teaspoons of salt
One teaspoon of ground black pepper
One teaspoon of ground cayenne pepper
Vegetable oil, olive oil, or butter
Lemon wedges

Wha' Cha' Do:

Rinse the fish filets under cold water and dry thoroughly with paper towels.
Lay them in a dish and pour the milk on top of them. In another dish, combine the cornmeal, salt, black and cayenne pepper. Remove the filets one at
a time from the milk, roll in the cornmeal mixture, and place on a large
platter, leaving space in between them. Let them dry at least five minutes.
Heat the oil or butter in a large frying pan. Add the filets and cook them for

five to seven minutes on a side, sprinkling with additional salt after each turn. Cook until golden brown and the fish flakes easily with a fork. Drain on paper towels. After draining, place them onto another platter covered with paper towels and put them into a preheated oven to keep them warm while frying the remaining filets. They will remain hot and crisp for as long as 35 minutes. Serve with lemon wedges. Serves four.

SEASONED MUSSELS (ANCIENT ROME)

The ancient Romans used lots of galley slaves, and galley slaves developed lots of muscles from rowing them around. Inductive (or is it deductive?) reasoning tells us that the ancient Romans had a ready supply of muscles, which  has absolutely nothing to do with this recipe … but its preparation will probably lead to meeting your downwind neighbors. So here is the original recipe straight out of an ancient Roman cookbook. (Recipe courtesy of ol' Marcus Gavius Apicius again)

Wha' Cha' Need:

Large boiling pot

40 to 50 fresh live mussels
Two tablespoons of *garum* (see note)
½ cup of wine
½ cup of *passum* (see second note)
One leek, chopped
A handful of fresh cumin and savory, minced

About Garum:

Also called *liquamen*, this was a popular fish sauce that ancient Romans made by fermenting fatty fish in brine and adding other flavorings. Connoisseurs insist that the best garum is from the blood, gills, and other guts of tuna. You could experiment with using Asian fish sauces like the Vietnamese *Nuoc Mam* or Thai *Nam Pla*, but I suspect that a gourmet like yourself will prefer to whip up a batch of your very own garum using that old family recipe of Grandpa Claudius.

About Passum:

This is a thick, syrupy wine. I would probably just substitute something like the Italian dessert wine *Vin Santo*, but you can make your own passum by boiling a pint of cheap wine until the volume is reduced by half, then adding honey to sweeten its to your taste.

Wha' Cha' Do:

Wash the mussels thoroughly to remove any sand. Boil them along with all of the remaining ingredients in sufficient water to cover until the mussels open, and discard any that refuse to do so. Serves four. *E pluribus Eatum!*

SHRIMP ON THE BARBIE (AUSTRALIA)

In 1986, the Australian Tourist Commission ran a television commercial that featured comedian and actor Paul Hogan (a.k.a. Crocodile Dundee). The actual closing line was "I'll slip another shrimp on the barbie for you," but it frequently is misquoted as "throw" or "put." While "barbie" is their slang term for barbeque, Aussies invariably use the term "prawn" instead of "shrimp." But because the commercial was intended for American television, the substitution was made.

Wha' Cha' Need:

Large mixing bowl
Barbeque grill
Skewers

½ cup of butter, melted
¼ cup of olive oil
¼ cup of minced fresh herbs (parsley, thyme, and cilantro)
Three tablespoons of fresh lemon juice
Three large garlic cloves, crushed
One tablespoon of minced shallot
Salt and pepper, freshly ground
One and ½ pounds of large shrimp, unpeeled
Fresh Spinach Leaves

Wha' Cha' Do:

Combine the first eight ingredients in large bowl. Mix in the shrimp. Marinate at room temperature for about one hour or in the refrigerator for five hours, stirring occasionally. Prepare the barbecue with medium-hot coals. Thread the shrimp onto skewers. Grill until the shrimp are just opaque, about two minutes per side. Line the serving plates with fresh spinach leaves. Serves eight.

STUFFED SOLE (LAKE TAHOE, CA)

Tahoe is home to many meticulously restored wooden boats, including the sleek Italian Rivas and those built by the American engineer and industrialist Garfield Wood. The latter owned the fastest powerboat in the world back in 1933, when four supercharged Packard engines pushed his *Miss America X* to 102 miles per hour. *Garwood's Grill & Pier* on the North Shore and *The Riva Grill* on the South Shore celebrate these classic "woodies," and are quite popular among Lake Tahoe boaters. Here is a recipe for one of their signature dishes, courtesy of Chef Peter.

Note—It may not be wise to attempt this dish in a one-pot, one-burner, galley.

Wha' Cha' Need:

Two saucepans

The Fish Dish:
Two ounces of shallots, chopped
One ounce of olive oil
Three ounces of raw lobster meat
Two ounces of sherry wine
One cup of heavy cream
Six ounces of Dungeness crabmeat
One teaspoon of Old Bay seasoning
One bunch of green onions, chopped
One whole egg
One and ½ pounds of Petrale, Dover, or English Sole

The Tomato Coulis:
One ounce of garlic, chopped
One ounce of olive oil
Two ounces of white wine
Two pounds of Roma tomatoes, chopped
Two cups of fish stock (or chicken stock, or water)

One ounce of tomato paste
½ bunch of fresh basil

Another Note—For folks with plastic boats or plastic heads, "coulis" is the French term for a pureed sauce or flavoring agent often used to decorate dishes like this.

Wha' Cha' Do:

The Fish Dish:
Wilt the shallots in olive oil over medium heat in a saucepan. Chop the raw lobster meat up into small chunks. Sauté the lobster chunks in the saucepan then de-glaze it with the sherry wine. Remove the lobster chunks from the pan when they are cooked medium-rare. Add the heavy cream to the saucepan and reduce. Drain the water from the crabmeat. When the cream has reduced down to ¼ its original amount and is thick, mix in the Old Bay seasoning, remove the mixture from the heat and fold in the crab and lobster meat, green onions, and egg then let the mixture cool. Remove any bones from the fish and cut it into four equal portions. Fill each portion of fish with an equal amount of stuffing then roll. Place the rolled fish portions into a greased baking pan, and bake at 325 degrees F for about seven to ten minutes until fish is done and the stuffing reaches a temperature of 140 degree F.

The Tomato Coulis:
While the fish is baking, wilt the chopped garlic in olive oil over medium heat in a saucepan. Deglaze the pan with white wine, add the Roma tomatoes, fish stock, and tomato paste, and reduce this mixture by one-half. Remove it from the heat, add the basil, and puree. Spoon the warm coulis onto the bottom of the serving plates, and top with the rolled fish portions. Serves four.

WALLEYE SUPREME (MINNESOTA)

Walleye is a mild-flavored freshwater game fish native to northern lakes. It has been the state fish of Minnesota since 1965, and its name comes from the fact that they can see well in low-light conditions. Local anglers commonly look for a good "walleye chop" (i.e., rough water), because their eyes let these fish increase their feeding activity under such conditions. Many people consider them to be one of the finest tasting of all freshwater fish, and I am not going to argue with that. Walleye recipes can be as simple as wrapping filets in aluminum foil with some butter, salt, pepper, and lemon juice and grilling them over a campfire to the following supremely delicious dish:

Wha' Cha' Need:

Shallow baking dish
Mixing bowl

One pound of walleye filets, about ¾ inch thick
One medium-sized sweet onion, diced
Eight ounces of cheddar cheese, grated
Eight ounces of sour cream
One (10½ ounce) can of cream of mushroom soup

Wha' Cha' Do:

Preheat your oven to 350 degree F. Place the filets into a shallow baking pan that has been lightly coated with non-stick cooking spray. Spread the diced onion and cheddar cheese evenly on top of the fish. Mix the sour cream and the cream of mushroom soup together in a bowl and spoon it over the fish. Bake it in the preheated oven for about 30 to 35 minutes. Serves four.

FEEDIN' THE FLEET

BOOYAH (GREEN BAY, WI)

During the 1800s, many settlers came to the Upper Midwest aboard Mississippi steamboats and Great Lakes steamers. Some say that this hearty stew was first introduced by Walloon Belgian settlers in Wisconsin, while others insist that it originated with Balloon Welgian settlers in Bisconsin. Its odd name apparently comes from "bouillir," a French word that means, "to boil." Cheeseheads have made it ever since, and most claim that booyah goes beautifully with beer.

Wha' Cha' Need:

Big deep kettle
Large serving bowls

One stewing chicken (about 4 pounds)
One pound of beef stew meat, with bones
One pound of pork stew meat, with bones
½ cup of minced parsley
One tablespoon of salt
One tablespoon of rosemary
One tablespoon of thyme
½ teaspoon of pepper
½ teaspoon of sage
Four cups of potatoes, quartered
Two cups of onions, chopped

Two cups of celery, chopped
One cup of carrots, cut up
One cup of green beans, cut up
One cup of fresh peas
One cup of tomatoes, skinned, seeded, & chopped
Two whole lemons

Wha' Cha' Do:

Put the chicken, beef, and pork into a deep kettle, and cover with boiling water. Slowly bring it to a simmer, remove any scum from the top, and add the herbs and seasonings. Cover and simmer very gently for about one hour. Remove the chicken, and when it has cooled, take the meat from the bones and cut it into pieces. Allow the beef and the pork continue to cook until tender, for about 45 minutes to an hour more. Remove, let cool, and remove the meat from bones. Add the vegetables to the broth and simmer for ten to fifteen minutes. Grate the lemon rind and set it aside. Remove the white pith and seeds from the lemons, chop up the pulp, and add the latter to the broth. Taste for seasoning. While the vegetables are still crisp, return the meat pieces to the broth to heat thoroughly. Serve it in large soup bowls and sprinkle with the grated lemon rind. Serves between twelve and sixteen hungry Walloons.

BURGOO (OWENSBORO, KY)

Before you Kentucky boaters get too smug, you should be aware that European sailors in the 17th Century had a similar name for a porridge made from bulgur wheat and other grains. Many say that today's burgoo capital is Owensboro on the Ohio River. This dish is quite popular during the Derby, and is often eaten like a dip with saltine crackers. Although there is no universal recipe, most of them share at least four similarities: meat, vegetables, a thickening agent, and very long cooking time. If you need to feed about 20 people, have the following ingredients and about three days, you might want to try this burgoo recipe.

Wha' Cha' Need:

Large stockpot(s)
Storage pan(s)
Roasting pans or Dutch oven(s)

Five pounds (uncooked boned weight) of beef chuck and/or pork butt roast(s)
Italian seasoning
Salt to taste
Three pounds of potatoes
One pound of carrots
One (28 ounce) can of crushed tomatoes
One (16 ounce) jar of medium salsa
One small onion
Canola oil
One (eight-ounce) can of tomato sauce
½ cup of brown sugar
¼ cup of hickory smoke barbeque sauce
One can of whole kernel corn
One can of green beans
One bag of frozen lima beans
One bag of frozen okra (optional)
One large can of tomato or V8 juice

Wha' Cha' Do:

The First Day:
Cut the beef chuck and/or pork butt roast(s) into ¾ inch thick slices. If you include both, use roughly the same amounts of beef and pork. After adding the salt and Italian seasoning to the water, simmer the beef and pork in separate stockpots for about 45 minutes, or until the meat comes off of the bones easily. Remove all of the bones from the meat after boiling, place the beef and pork into separate pans, and refrigerate. Also save and refrigerate the boiling stock liquid for use on the second day.

The Second Day:
Peel and dice the potatoes, and cut the carrots into small slices. Take the previous day's stock out of the refrigerator and discard any white fat layer that may have formed on its top surface. Reserve a third of the stock, and put the remaining two-thirds into a large pot with the diced potatoes, sliced carrots, and a little more salt. Stir in the crushed tomatoes, and cook the mixture for around 20 minutes, or until the vegetables are slightly undercooked. Return the mixture to the refrigerator.

Remove the meat(s) from the refrigerator, place into separate roasting pans, and add a little of the reserved stock. Cover the pans lightly with foil, and roast for at least three hours at 300 degrees F. Periodically check and add stock to keep the meat from drying out. Chop up a small onion and brown it in Canola Oil. After an hour and a half, spoon the chopped onion and the medium salsa over the beef. At about the same time, cover the pork with a mixture of the tomato sauce, brown sugar, and barbeque sauce. Return the meat(s) to the oven, and continue roasting for another hour and a half. When done, return the roasted meat(s) to the refrigerator for use on the third day.

The Third Day:

For the final day of cooking, you can use a Dutch oven style roaster, a large turkey roaster that will fit into your oven, or several crock-pots. You will also need at least three hours, so if you plan to serve at 5 p.m. you will need to begin around 2 p.m. Combine the potato-carrot-tomato mixture with the meat(s), and add the whole kernel corn, green beans, lima beans, okra (if you use any), and the tomato/V8 juice. Cook it all together for another three hours at 275 to 300 degrees F, stirring occasionally. Serve with corn-bread or corn muffins on the side. Enjoy, because you earned it! Serves about twenty.

HAVANA BARBEQUE (CUBA)

Compared to Burgoo, this recipe practically makes itself … and it only takes two days! But if you eat too much of it, you may begin to talk like Desi Arnaz, pick up a conga drum, and begin singing "Ba-Ba-Loo!"

Wha' Cha' Need:

Large mixing bowl
Large re-sealable plastic bag
Re-sealable plastic bag(s)
Large cooking pot
Serving bowls

24 ounces of barbecue sauce
¼ cup of Tabasco sauce
One and ½ cups of olive oil
One cup of yellow onion, finely minced
Six cloves of garlic, peeled, finely minced
½ tablespoon of ground cayenne pepper
One teaspoon of salt
Three tablespoons of ground black pepper
Four pounds of roast pork loin, very thinly sliced
Two pounds of smoked ham, very thinly sliced

Four large tomatoes, cored, seeded, & diced
2/3 cup of distilled white vinegar
Four tablespoons of fresh parsley, chopped
¼ pound (one stick) of salted butter
20 to 24 slices of yellow cheddar cheese
Fresh sliced white bread, remove and save crusts
Scallions or green onions, very finely diced

Wha' Cha' Do:

Combine the barbeque sauce, Tabasco, olive oil, onion, garlic and all of the other dry ingredients. Cover this sauce mixture and let it stand at room temperature for two to six hours. Place the meat slices and sauce mixture into a re-sealable bag, slowly add the tomatoes and vinegar, seal the bag tightly, and rotate it to coat all of the meat with the liquid. Place the bag into the refrigerator overnight, turning and kneading it every few hours. Remove the bag from the refrigerator and pour the meat and liquid into a large cooking pot. Add the chopped parsley and butter and bring it to a slow boil, stirring frequently. Cover it and reduce the heat to a slow simmer for 60 minutes, stirring thoroughly every so often. Spoon some of the warm mixture over a slice of white bread in a serving bowl, add a slice of cheese, and then a second slice of bread. Dip more of the sauce over the top, add some bread crusts into each bowl, and garnish with very finely chopped scallions or green onions. Eat with a fork using the bread as a sop. Serves 20 to 24 hungry Cubanos.

S.O.S. (UNITED STATES NAVY)

Landlubbers call this dish *creamed sliced dried beef on toast*, but we swabbies have a more colorful name for it. The first word in that case is not "stuff," but the last word is "shingle." The Fleet's in, so it's time to open all the bars and hide all the (pretty) women. (Recipe courtesy of the United States Navy)

Wha' Cha' Need:

Large cooking containers

Two pounds of butter or shortening
Two and ½ pounds of flour, sifted
One tablespoon of ground black pepper
Four and ¾ gallons of whole milk, hot
Seven pounds of dried beef, thinly sliced
One more pound of butter or shortening
Toast, rice, noodles, or baked potatoes

Wha' Cha' Do:

Melt the first two pounds of butter or shortening, add in the flour, and blend them together. Add the black pepper, and cook the mixture for five minutes. Add the hot milk slowly, stirring to prevent lumps. Separate the dried beef into slices, and cook them in the remaining pound of hot butter or shortening until the edges curl. If the beef is too salty, soak it in hot water for about 15 minutes instead of cooking it in the hot butter/shortening. After draining the meat, add it to the sauce, and blend thoroughly. Serve it over toast, steamed rice, noodles, or baked potatoes. Makes six and ¼ gallons, or roughly 100 one-cup portions.

VEGGIE VICTUALS

Vessels operating in coastal waters were sometimes able to go ashore to replenish their stores of fresh fruit and vegetables, while the diets of those aboard vessels on long voyages were dominated by pickled, canned, or dried items (e.g., beans).

BAKED BEANS (BOSTON, MA)

Have you ever wondered why Boston is nicknamed "Beantown?" The nickname can be traced back to when New England was a key leg on the "triangle trade" of African slaves, Caribbean molasses, and American rum. At one point there were 63 distilleries in Massachusetts, and most of them were in the Boston area. This entailed storing lots of molasses that could either be fermented into "demon rum" or added to baked beans. The latter caused so much local pressure that by 1910 folks proclaimed, "You don't know beans until you come to Boston." But tragedy struck in 1919, when a gigantic storage tank burst, sending a five-foot high wall of molasses down the streets and killing a dozen horses, one cat, and 21 people. Bostonians bailed themselves out of the sticky situation by eating more beans. Traditional Saturday night meals still include baked beans, and "Bean Suppers" are still popular fundraisers for schools, churches, and civic organizations.

Wha' Cha' Need:

Soaking/cooking pots
Bean pot or casserole
Mixing bowl

Enough water to cover the beans
One pound of dry navy beans
¼ pound of salt pork, cut into chunks
¼ cup of brown sugar
One teaspoon of dry mustard
Two teaspoons of chopped onion
½ cup of dark molasses
One and ½ teaspoons of salt

Wha' Cha' Do:

Soak the beans overnight. Bring them to a boil in the same water and simmer until tender, for about 1½ to 2 hours. Drain them, reserving the liquid. Preheat the oven to 275 degrees F. Place the beans and salt pork chunks into a bean pot or casserole. Combine the reserved cooking liquid, brown sugar, dry mustard, chopped onion, dark molasses, and salt; and pour it over beans. Cover and bake for three to four hours. Makes six to eight servings.

BAKED BREADFRUIT (HAWAII)

Breadfruit, or *ulu* in Hawaiian, has a colorful history and reputation. Its wood was used to make drums, canoes, and surfboards; its rough foliage was used to polish kukui nuts, and its fruit was a key part of many Polynesian diets. By the 18th century, rumors of super-strong Pacific islanders who lived upon breadfruit reached England at a time when they were seeking ways to boost the productivity of African slaves in the British West Indies. In 1787, the *HMS Bounty* under the command of William Bligh was sent to Tahiti to bring a thousand breadfruit tree saplings to the Caribbean. But by the second leg of their voyage, the crew had started to take a dim view of giving up their precious fresh water to a bunch of plants, so they set Captain Bligh and some of his loyalists adrift (and I'll bet you thought that the mutiny had something to do with half-naked Tahitian women). For many years Hawaiians have baked breadfruit whole over open fires, turning them over with sticks until they became soft inside. They scraped off the charred outer skins with shells or pieces of broken glass then broke off pieces and dipped them into coconut milk that was cooked with limejuice. Here is an easier recipe.

Wha' Cha' Need:

Baking pan
Aluminum foil
Shallow bowl

One ripe breadfruit (the skin will be yellow/brown, and the flesh soft)
¼ cup of butter
Three tablespoons of brown sugar
One cup of water

Wha' Cha' Do:

Wash a ripe breadfruit and remove the core by pulling the stem. Trim off the top edge if needed. Fill the cavity with butter and brown sugar. Cover it with foil and place it into a baking pan with a cup of water (to prevent scorching). Bake it for one hour at 350 degrees F. To serve, unwrap the breadfruit and cut it in half lengthwise. Bring it to the table in a shallow bowl with a large spoon. Scoop the breadfruit out with a large spoon to serve, making sure that each piece is topped with some of the sugar and butter.

BEAN-HOLE BEANS (MAINE)

The Penobscot Indians introduced early settlers to the practice of cooking beans with maple syrup and bits of meat in pots buried in the ground, and "bean-hole beans" remains a regional favorite that is often served at community events and family gatherings. Mainers typically use Yellow Eye, Jacob's Cattle, or Soldier Beans, but you can try other varieties. (Recipe courtesy of the Penobscots)

Wha' Cha' Need:

Shovel, Firewood
Cooking Pot, Heavy Dutch Oven
Wet dishcloth or towel

Water
Two quarts of dry beans
One large onion, sliced
One cup of dark molasses
Two slabs of salt pork/bacon

Wha' Cha' Do:

Dig a hole in the ground that is large enough to hold your Dutch oven and allow three inches of clearance on the sides and at least six inches of clearance on top. Save the dirt. Build a fire in the hole, and let it burn down to embers. While this is happening, parboil the beans until their skins wrinkle then drain off the liquid. Slice the onion, and put half of the slices into the Dutch oven. Pour in half of the beans, and put the rest of the onions slices and salt pork/bacon on top of them. Add the remaining beans, pour the dark molasses over them, and add enough water to cover the mixture. After the fire has burned down to embers, shovel enough out to make room for the Dutch oven, and place it (uncovered) into the bean hole. Lay the wet dishcloth/towel over the top of the Dutch oven, and push the lid down on top of the wet cloth. Shovel embers back around the sides and on top of the Dutch oven, and cover it with the dirt that you removed from the hole. Let it cook for about six hours. Serves four.

CHARLIE'S CHOKES (MOSS LANDING, CA)

When Captain Charlie Moss arrived, the area near the mouth of the Salinas River was already the site of commercial fishing, oyster farming, and whaling activities. The pier and shore facilities he built there turned Moss Landing into a busy port that shipped local agricultural products to the boomtown of San Francisco. This included raw sugar hauled in on Claus Spreckels' little narrow gauge railroad the locals called "The Dinky Line." Sardine fishing continued for awhile after most of Charlie's facilities were destroyed in the 1906 earthquake, but when the Italian farmers in nearby Castroville introduced artichokes, local agriculture turned its attention to the demands of folks who eat flower buds from giant thistle plants.

Wha' Cha' Need:

Sauté pan

Two pounds of baby artichokes
2/3 of a sweet onion, chopped
Two cloves of garlic, minced
Some extra virgin olive oil
Dry Italian seasoning
¾ cup of dry white wine
Packet of chicken bullion
Salt and pepper to taste
Linguini, cooked and drained
Freshly grated Parmesan cheese

Wha' Cha' Do:

Trim, clean, and cut the baby artichokes in half. Sauté the chopped onion and minced garlic in olive oil, add the baby artichoke halves, dry Italian seasoning, white wine, and chicken bullion. Next add the cooked pasta, and toss it together well. Salt and pepper to taste, and top it with plenty of grated Parmesan cheese.

GAZPACHO (ANDALUCIA, SPAIN)

The roots of this famous dish can be traced all of the way back to when Roman expeditionary forces carried rations of bread, salt, garlic, vinegar, and olive oil. Legionnaires combined these with local ingredients according to their personal tastes. For nearly 800 years Moors occupied the southern part of Spain that is now known as Andalucia, and they contributed to the evolution of what we call gazpacho. Day laborers used it to quench their thirsts and to keep going on hot summer days. The first version (*ajo blanco*) was white, and included almonds but no tomatoes. Christopher Columbus took barrels of this on his first voyage, but the introduction of tomatoes from the New World led to the red version that is best known today. Gazpacho should be served chilled, and may be drunk or eaten as: a cold soup, a liquid salad, a mid-morning snack, an appetizer, an afternoon refresher, or an evening's supper; and leftovers can be used as a dressing for salad or a topping for pasta.

Wha' Cha' Need:

Mixing bowl(s)
Mortar & pestle
Blender (optional)
Large bowl/pitcher
Four serving bowls
Six garnish bowls

El Dish:
Some Water
Four ounces of day-old white bread crumbs, without crusts
Two cloves of garlic, peeled
Two teaspoons of salt
Two and ¼ pounds of ripe tomatoes, peeled and seeded
One green bell pepper, cut into eighths
Two tablespoons of sherry wine vinegar
Five ounces of extra virgin olive oil

Los Garnishes:
One ripe but firm tomato, peeled and finely chopped
Two ounces of cucumber, peeled and finely chopped
Two ounces of green pepper, finely chopped
One small onion, peeled and finely chopped
Four ounces of day-old bread, diced
One hard-boiled egg, diced

Wha' Cha' Do:

Soak the breadcrumbs in a bowl of water. Squeeze off any excess water until the bread has a spongy texture. Pound the garlic and salt together in a mortar and liquefy it with a little water. If making it by hand use a round bowl. If you are using a blender, pour in the garlic/salt mixture; add the tomatoes, green bell pepper, and sherry wine vinegar; and blend. Slowly add the olive oil so that it emulsifies and the mixture thickens and becomes creamy. Check the seasoning and add more salt or vinegar if needed. Pour the mixture into a serving bowl or pitcher, cover, and refrigerate. Place the gazpacho in the center of the table surrounded by the garnishes in individual small bowls. Serves four.

GRITS AND CHEESE SOUFFLÉ (CAROLINA)

To most Yankees, grits first appear to be another one of several semi-edibles that are consumed south of the Mason-Dixon Line. They are sometimes mistaken for Cream of Wheat, until a local covers them with butter and gravy. Some say that they taste like whatever you put on them, but true southerners proclaim, "Dem grits might be tasteless, but so are some of dem folks dat hates 'em!"

Wha' Cha' Need:

Saucepan
Casserole dish

One cup of real (not them there instant) grits
One cup of sharp Cheddar cheese, shredded
¼ cup of whole milk
Four eggs, well beaten
½ teaspoon of baking powder
Salt, pepper, & garlic to taste
Dash of Tabasco (optional)

Wha' Cha' Do:

Cook the grits according to the directions on that there package. Whup 'em up with the remaining ingredients and pour the whole dang mixture into a greased one and ½ quart casserole dish. Bake it at 400 degrees F for about 30 minutes. Season to taste. Serves four to six True Grits.

PAPAYA FRITTERS (THE VIRGIN ISLANDS)

This oblong fruit with golden-yellow skin may have originally come from Central America or southern Mexico, but it has been grown in tropical regions around the world ever since the beginning of recorded history. Large papayas can get up to two feet long and can weigh as much as 25 pounds. Their flesh is used in juices, salads, and desserts; and the unripe fruit can be cooked like squash. Their skin contains a digestive enzyme called papain that is often used in meat tenderizers. When making the following recipe choose slightly unripe papayas with greenish yellow or greenish-orange skins, and please do not fret over these fritters.

Wha' Cha' Need:

Mixing bowl
Deep fryer or grill

½ cup of whole milk
One fresh egg, beaten
One cup of self-rising flour
Grated fresh nutmeg (optional)
One and ½ tablespoons of sugar
One cup of papaya, peeled and cut into cubes
Vegetable oil, for deep fat frying

Wha' Cha' Do:

Combine the milk, egg, flour, (nutmeg, if used), and sugar in a bowl. Add the papaya cubes and toss them to coat. Drop teaspoonfuls these cubes into hot oil, and cook them for one to two minutes on each side or until golden brown. Drain them on paper towels. Fritters can also be cooked on a grill, similar to a pancake. Serve them hot as a snack or as a side dish.

Note—Some people may find this dish to be a bit bland. Suggested seasonings include coriander, cardamom, or saffron; or you could top them with powdered sugar and eat them for dessert.

PATACONES (PANAMA)

Panama is sometimes called "the crossroads of the world," and it is famous for its canal, howler monkeys, and mosquitoes. I spent time there awhile back courtesy of the United States Navy, and also got stranded on an island with some wild pigs … but that's another story. You cannot talk about Panamanian cuisine without mentioning the plantain, or *plataño* in Spanish. These are much more than just bananas on steroids. They are the most plentiful vegetables in the country, and Panamanians eat truckloads each day. But you might be disappointed if you try to peel and eat them like bananas, because plantains must be cooked. Here is a recipe for fried green ones called *patacones*, which seem to be sold on every street corner and in every restaurant in Panama.

Note—Plantains were especially useful aboard ships because they did not ripen and spoil quickly, and could be baked into a nutritious starchy treat.

Wha' Cha' Need:

Frying pan
Rolling pin or bottle

Three medium-size green plantains
Some vegetable cooking oil
One teaspoon of salt
Ketchup (optional)

Wha' Cha' Do:

Peel the plantains (a potato peeler works well), and cut them into ½ inch thick slices. Fry these slices in a pan containing some hot oil until they are golden brown. Place them onto a cutting board, and smash them with a rolling pin, bottle, meat tenderizer hammer, hand sledge, etc. Sprinkle them with salt, return them to the pan, and fry them until they are crispy. Drain them upon paper towels and serve (with ketchup if desired). Makes six to eight servings.

POLENTA (VENICE, ITALY)

When Roman Legions set out to conquer the known world, a staple in their diets was *pulmentum*, a coarsely ground meal made from wild grain, primitive wheat, millet, chickpeas, etc. Mixed with water, it was eaten as porridge or baked into hard cakes on hot stones. Although bread was available in big cities like Rome, Legionnaires and the poor were more likely to have polenta. During the 15th or 16th centuries, Italians began making it out of maize brought back from the New World. It was not as nutritious as earlier versions, but polenta made from corn was more profitable for landowners. Its popularity gradually spread across Italy and to the Americas. It is extremely versatile, and can be served instead of bread or pasta, as a side dish, grilled, or in cake form.

Wha' Cha' Need:

Cooking pot
Large sheet pan

One tablespoon of salt
Eight cups of water
Two cups of corn meal
½ cup of real butter
One teaspoon of salt
¼ teaspoon of crushed red pepper
¼ teaspoon of ground black pepper
One and ½ cups of Reggiano cheese, shredded
Olive oil

Wha' Cha' Do:

Dissolve one tablespoon of salt into eight cups of water, and bring it to a rapid boil in a cooking pot. Pour the corn meal into the boiling salt water, and stir it with a whisk. Add the butter, one teaspoon of salt, both red and black pepper, and Reggiano cheese, and mix together. After the ingredients are thoroughly combined, reduce the heat to medium, and continue to cook it for roughly 45 minutes while stirring constantly. Pour it into a large sheet pan, and spread it evenly to cool. After it has hardened (about 20 minutes), cut it into serving-size squares. Just before serving, brush the squares with olive oil and brown both sides on a preheated grill. Serve plain or with a sauce of your choice.

RED BEANS AND RICE (SLIDELL, LA)

The first time that I encountered this dish, I thought it resembled a glutinous mass of molten bricks with occasional lumps. It illustrates that time-honored principle of southern cooking, which is, "y'all cook everything til it's done, then keep on a-cookin' it for at least four more hours." Even if you do not happen to be in Louisiana for this traditional Monday dish, you will find that it tastes a lot better than it looks.

Wha' Cha' Need:

Large pot

One pound of dried red beans
Two large onions, chopped
Two stalks of celery, chopped
One medium-size green pepper, chopped
One clove of garlic, minced
Two teaspoons of salt
½ teaspoon of pepper
¼ cup of chopped parsley
Hot cooked rice
Two pounds of smoked sausage

Wha' Cha' Do:

Wash the beans. Combine the beans, onions, celery, green pepper, and garlic in a large pot, cover with water, and bring it to a boil. Reduce the heat, cover, and simmer for 2 to 2½ hours, or until the beans are tender and turn into a thick gravy. If needed, add more water to prevent the beans from sticking. Stir in the salt, pepper, and parsley. Cook the sausage until it is done and cut it into serving-size pieces. Mound a passle of cooked rice in the middle of serving plates. Spoon the beans around the rice, and place the sausage pieces onto the plates. Serves eight to ten.

RICE AND PEAS (JAMAICA)

No Sunday dinner in Jamaica is complete without rice and peas. Most of the time it is prepared using what Jamaicans call "red peas" (a.k.a. kidney beans), but for Christmas dinners they absolutely must be green *gungo*, or pigeon peas. Often eaten with jerk dishes, some versions call for more "peas" while others use a salted pig's tail to add flavoring. However, most recipes include seasoning with Scotch Bonnet (Habañero) pepper and coconut milk. Try this one and you might say, "Ya, dat's good eatin', mon!"

Wha' Cha' Need:

Cooking pot(s)

One cup of dried kidney beans
One cup of coconut milk
Four cups of water
Two garlic cloves, bruised
Two sprigs of fresh thyme
Two scallions
Two strips of bacon
One whole green Scotch Bonnet (Habañero) pepper
Salt and pepper to taste
Two cups of white rice

Wha' Cha' Do:

Soak the dried beans in water overnight to soften. Cook the soaked beans in a mixture of the coconut milk, water, garlic, thyme, scallion, and the whole green Scotch Bonnet (Habañero) pepper just until they are tender. Add the bacon, salt, and pepper; and taste for seasoning. If it is too spicy, remove the Scotch Bonnet (Habañero) pepper. Add the rice, and simmer over low heat for 40 minutes until the rice is tender and the liquids have been absorbed. If necessary, add more water while the dish is cooking. Remove the sprigs of thyme, scallions, and bacon before serving. Serves six to eight.

Tips—If the "peas" are overcooked before adding the rice they will be mushy. The amount of liquid for the final cooking should be roughly 2 to 2½ times as much as the amount of rice and peas. If there is too much liquid in the pot when you add the rice, take some out and reserve it to add later if the rice dries out before it's done.

KNEAD SOME DOUGH?

Mariners have long faced the need for nutritious, easy to stow, easy to transport, and long-lasting food. Nuts, rice, dried fruit and vegetables were all staples, but the advent of baking various cereal crops provided another important food source for seafarers. Early Egyptian vessels often carried *dhourra*, a flat brittle loaf of maize bread. The Romans had a biscuit that they called *buccellum,* and when King Richard the Lionhearted left on the Third Crusade back in 1189, he took along *biskits* made out of corn, barley, rye, and bean flour.

CREOLE CORNBREAD (NEW ORLEANS, LA)

Cajuns can trace their ancestry back to the Acadians from Nova Scotia, while Creoles were descendants of French and Spanish settlers and African slaves who worked on colonial plantations. Most Cajuns settled in rural areas of southern Louisiana, but Creoles preferred more urban surroundings. Some say that one of the most famous Creoles besides Jelly Roll Morton and Marie Leveau was the dashing privateer (or was it pirate?) Jean Lafitte. With headquarters in the French Quarter, he established his own little kingdom of *Barataria* in the nearby bayous. He never  attacked an American ship, and provided men to help Andrew Jackson fight the British during the Battle of New Orleans. Lafitte later moved to

Galveston, TX where he lived in a combination fortress/mansion. After being forced to leave there, Lafitte seemingly vanished. Some claim that he died off of Yucatan, while others say that he headed up the Mississippi River to near St. Louis where he lived quietly until the 1840s. Think of him when you fix this Creole cornbread.

Wha' Cha' Need:

Two mixing bowls
Ten-inch cast iron skillet

Two cups of cooked rice
One cup of yellow cornmeal
½ cup of chopped onion
One to two tablespoons of seeded and chopped Jalapeños
One teaspoon of salt
½ teaspoon of baking soda
Two whole eggs
One cup of whole milk
¼ cup of vegetable oil
One (16½ ounce) can of cream-style corn
Three cups (12 ounces) of shredded cheddar cheese
A little extra cornmeal

Wha' Cha' Do:

Combine the cooked rice, cornmeal, chopped onion, chopped Jalapeños, salt, and baking soda in a large mixing bowl. In a second bowl, beat the eggs, milk, and oil, add the creamed corn, and mix it well. Combine this with the earlier rice mixture, and fold in the shredded cheddar cheese to complete the batter. Next sprinkle a well-greased ten-inch cast iron skillet with some extra cornmeal then pour in the batter. Bake it at 350 degrees F for about 45 to 50 minutes or until the cornbread tests done. Serve it with lots of butter and honey. Serves 12.

CRUMPETS (ENGLAND)

The word crumpet can be traced as far back as 1382, and the first written recipe for a *crompid cake* appeared in the 17th Century. Although similar to so-called "English muffins," crumpets are made from different dough (and you do not have to split them in half). They are traditionally baked on cast iron griddles in special metal crumpet rings, and are often served toasted as part of High Tea with neat cucumber and salmon sandwiches and small iced cakes. Cheerio, old chap!

Wha' Cha' Need:

Flour sifter
Mixing bowls
Frying pan or griddle
Crumpet rings or pastry cutters

One and ½ pounds of flour
One teaspoon of salt
One tablespoon of dried yeast
One and ¾ pints of milk

Wha' Cha' Do:

Sift the flour and salt into a mixing bowl. Dissolve the yeast into one-half cup of warmed milk then set this mixture aside in a warm place until the yeast begins to work (a brownish froth will appear on the surface after about five minutes). Make a well in the center of the flour, pour the warm milk and yeast mixture into it then add the rest of the warmed milk. Beat it vigorously to incorporate air into the mixture until it becomes a thick batter. Cover the batter and place it aside in a warm place to rise for about 45 minutes.

Thoroughly grease a frying pan or cast iron griddle and place it over high heat. Grease the insides of three or four crumpet rings or plain metal pastry cutters. Place the rings onto the hot surface and leave for about two minutes until they are very hot. Pour a little batter into each ring/cutter to a depth of about ½ inch. Cook for five to seven minutes until the tops appear dry and honeycombed with holes. Turn the crumpets out onto the pan/griddle and cook for another two to three minutes. Cool on a wire rack.

FRENCH TOAST (HANNIBAL, MO)

Located on the bank of the mighty Mississippi, Hannibal is a river town of many legends. There is Tom Sawyer, Becky Thatcher, Huckleberry Finn, and of course, Lula Belle's. Back in 1917 an enterprising Madam from Chicago built a bordello several blocks from Mark Twain's boyhood home, and it operated as such until the 1950s. Lula Belle's has subsequently become a popular bed & breakfast, offering rooms with such colorful names as: the Angel of Delight, Gypsy Rose, the Farmer's
Daughter, Bird of Paradise, and Purple Passion. Here is a recipe for one of their signature dishes, courtesy of Mike. And if you do not quite feel up to making it at home, you can always get a piece at Lula Belle's.

Wha' Cha' Need:

Mixing bowl
Baking sheet
Aluminum foil
Non-stick cooking spray

Le Batter:
Six fresh eggs
Two and ½ cups of whole milk
Cinnamon, nutmeg, & allspice
½ ounce of Amaretto or Calvados

Le Toast:
Loaf of day-old French bread
¾ stick of real butter, melted
Brown sugar
Powdered sugar

Wha' Cha' Do:

Le Batter:

In a mixing bowl, beat the eggs and milk together into a light batter. Add the cinnamon, nutmeg, and allspice to taste, along with a splash or two of the Amaretto or Calvados liquor.

Le Toast:

Spray a baking sheet with non-stick cooking spray. Liberally coat it with melted butter, and sprinkle the entire sheet generously with brown sugar. Cut the bread into twelve slices that are roughly ½ to one inch thick. Dip each slice into the batter, place onto the baking sheet, and cover with aluminum foil. Place the baking sheet into a preheated 350 degree F oven. Bake it for 20 minutes then remove the aluminum foil. Bake for an additional 15 minutes, or until the tops of the bread slices are brown and the brown sugar is caramelized. Garnish with powdered sugar and serve. Makes four servings.

Note—For your ~~regular~~ ~~customers~~ ~~clients~~ ~~patrons~~ special guests, you may want to serve this topped with fresh fruit.

HUSH PUPPIES (THE SOUTH)

The true origin of the name for this dish may never be known. Some insist that it originated from when southern fishermen, hunters, or Confederate soldiers threw bits of fried cornmeal dough to their dogs to keep them quiet. Others claim that the name came from the Louisiana swamps, where Cajuns fried up salamanders called "water puppies." The following recipe does not include any salamander meat, but you could add some if you happen to be on *The Amphibian Diet.*

Wha' Cha' Need:

Mixing bowl
Deep fryer

One egg
½ cup of milk
One cup of yellow stone-ground corn meal
Two to three teaspoons of minced onions
One teaspoon of baking powder
½ teaspoon of salt

Wha' Cha' Do:

Beat de egg into de milk. Add de corn meal, minced onions, baking powder, and salt, mix dis into a batter. Scoop de batter into de desired size for yo' hush puppies ('bouts two inches in diameter), drop dem into de deep fryer, and cook dem 'til dey is golden brown. Makes 'bout a dozen of de little rascals. *Sho' nuff!*

JOHNNY CAKES (COLONIAL VIRGINIA)

If folks in the Deep South made hush puppies to keep their dogs quiet, people in Virginia must have created these to shut up some motor mouth named Johnny. Some of our more boring historians say they came to be after Native Americans taught the colonists how to cook with cornmeal. The name might have evolved from "journey cakes" because they traveled well, but their other names include: Shawnee cakes, hoecakes, jonakin, and ashcakes. An early recipe for the latter called for wrapping the batter up in cabbage leaves, and burying it in the ashes toward the rear of one's fireplace. In any event, h-e-e-r-e-'s Johnny!

Wha' Cha' Need:

Mixing bowl
Frying pan

One cup of cornmeal
One teaspoon of salt
One teaspoon of sugar (optional)
One cup of boiling water
¼ to ½ cup of milk
Butter for frying

Wha' Cha' Do:

Combine the cornmeal, salt, and sugar (if used). Pour the boiling water over the top of this mixture, whisk it together to prevent lumps, and let this batter rest for ten minutes. Heat a buttered frying pan to around 375 degrees F over medium heat (butter should sizzle but not burn). Add enough milk to the earlier batter to reach the consistency of mashed potatoes, and drop spoonfuls of it into the frying pan to produce cakes that are roughly two to three inches in diameter. Flip them over when the bottoms get golden brown. Serve them warm with butter, honey, maple syrup, or other toppings. Makes about eight cakes.

SHIP'S BISCUITS (TRADITIONAL)

Also called hardtack, ship's biscuits have been around for centuries, and a typical daily ration for 16th century mariners included a pound of biscuits and a gallon of ale. At first the actual baking was done ashore, but by the mid-1800s it became possible to more safely bake aboard
ship. While recipes varied a little, most ship's biscuits were designed to be durable in the vessel's bread room. Double or triple baking made them quite hard, although stories of infestations of weevils or large maggots called "bargemen" are legendary. The mess decks on many of the ships back then were not that well lighted, which was probably a very good thing. For those of you who long to return to those days of wooden ships, iron men, and broken teeth; here is one recipe for a batch of durable ship's biscuits.

Wha' Cha' Need:

Mixing bowl
Rolling pin or bottle

Some water
One pound of flour
One teaspoon of salt

Note—It could be difficult to make historically authentic hardtack with today's refined flours, since most were produced using medium-coarse, stone-ground whole meal flour. So just do your best old chap, and cheerio!

Wha' Cha' Do:

Mix enough water into the flour and salt to make stiff dough. Leave it alone for about ½ hour, and roll it out until it is about ½ inch thick. Cut it into squares (to keep them from rolling about the deck), and pierce each several times with a fork. Bake in a 420 degree F oven for 30 to 45 minutes, and leave them in a warm dry place to further dry and harden. Best consumed with copious amounts of liquid.

SWEET THINGS

Pirates were not just a bunch of swarthy men with peg legs and eye patches ... some of them were women. Two of the most famous were Mary Read and Anne Bonny. Mary was an illegitimate child whose mother dressed her as a boy to impersonate her (deceased) legitimate brother, and thereby hide her mother's sexual indiscretions from her sea-faring husband. Mary spent most of her adult life posing as a man and eventually found herself on board the ship of the pirate "Calico Jack" Rackham, where she met his mistress Anne Bonny. Mary's gender eventually became known to the rest of the crew,  but both women were known as fierce fighters. They were both captured, but were given reprieves when it was learned that they were both pregnant. Isn't that sweet?

ACADIAN APPLES (NOVA SCOTIA)

The Scots were the first to lay claim to the land they called *Nova Scotia*, or "New Scotland." In 1497 England claimed the place, and about a century later a fleet of French vessels arrived and called the area *Acadie*, which means "fertile land." After the English took over again about a century later, many of the so-called Acadians were expelled, but here is one of their recipes.

Wha' Cha' Need:

Mixing bowl
Double boiler
Plastic wrap
Baking sheet
Toothpicks

The Vanilla Sauce:
One tablespoon of cornstarch
One teaspoon of cold water
One cup of heavy cream
½ cup of confectioner's sugar
½ teaspoon of vanilla extract

The Other Stuff:
Six medium-sized baking apples
One cup of whole-berry cranberry sauce
Four sheets of phyllo dough
2/3 cup of melted butter

Wha' Cha; Do:

The Vanilla Sauce
Mix the water and cornstarch together. Whisk the cream, confectioner's sugar, vanilla and the cornstarch mixture together until smooth. Heat it in the top of a double boiler, whisking constantly until the mixture thickens. Remove it from the heat, cover it with plastic wrap, and chill. Yields about one cup of sauce.

The Other Stuff:
Pre-heat the oven to 375 degrees F. Core the apples and score the skin around them. Loosely fill the apple cavities with the cranberry sauce. Brush each sheet of phyllo dough with melted butter. Place an apple onto each phyllo dough sheet, and fold the pastry up and around the apple. Turn the apple upside down and repeat the process with a second piece of phyllo dough. Return the apple to its upright position and apply the remaining

two sheets of pastry, folding the pastry from corner-to-corner and twisting the top to seal. Repeat the process with all of the remaining apples. Place the apples onto an ungreased baking sheet and bake them for about 20 to 30 minutes (depending upon the type of apple used). Test them for doneness using a toothpick. If it goes in smoothly, the apple is done. Place the apples on dessert plates and top with vanilla sauce. Serves six.

BAYOU GOO (CAJUN COUNTRY)

Real swamp mud is dark and rich just like this tasty dessert, and they are both pretty easy to make. Unlike the lumps in real bayou goo, the ones in this dish will not eat you … but they are nuts. (Recipe courtesy of Maw Maw)

Wha' Cha' Need:

Mixing bowls
Glass 9 by 13-inch baking dish

De Crust:
One cup of flour
½ cup of chopped pecans
One stick of softened butter

De Bottom Filllin':
One (8 ounce) package of cream cheese
Four to five ounces of Cool Whip
One cup of powdered sugar

De Middle Fillin':
Two (4 ounce) boxes of instant chocolate pudding mix
Two cups of whole milk

De Toppin':
Four to five more ounces of Cool Whip
¼ cup of pecan pieces

Wha' Cha' Do:

De Crust:
Combine de flour, chopped pecans, and softened butter; and press dis mixture onto de bottom and de sides of and glass 9 by 13-inch baking pan. Bake it at 350 degrees F for 20 to 30 minutes until de edges are golden brown. Remove from de oven and let it cool completely.

De Bottom Fillin':
Mix de cream cheese, Cool Whip, and powdered sugar together, and spread it on top of de completely cooled crust (see above).

De Middle Fillin':
Combine de instant chocolate pudding and whole milk, and pour dis mixture on top of de bottom fillin' (see above again).

De Toppin':
Top with de additional Cool Whip, garnish with de pecan pieces, and refrigerate 'til serving.

GOOEY BUTTER CAKE (ST. LOUIS, MO)

St. Louis began as a French trading post in 1764, but during the 1800s a large number of German immigrants came up the Mississippi from New Orleans and settled in the area because they saw similarities with Germany's wine country. This traditional St. Louis dish apparently began in the 1930s, when a German baker added the wrong proportions of ingredients to his cake batter. It turned into a rather gooey, but quite delicious, mess. Gooey butter cake is frequently served as a coffee cake, instead of as a dessert.

Wha' Cha' Need:

Mixing bowls
9 by 9 by 2-inch baking pan

The Crust:
One cup of all-purpose flour
Three tablespoons of sugar
1/3 cup of butter or margarine

The Filling:
One and ¼ cups of sugar
¾ cup of butter or margarine
One egg
One cup of all-purpose flour
2/3 cup of evaporated milk
¼ cup of light corn syrup
One teaspoon of vanilla extract
Powdered sugar

Wha' Cha' Do:

The Crust:

In mixing bowl, combine the flour and sugar. Cut in the butter/margarine until the mixture resembles fine crumbs and begins to cling. Pat onto the bottom and the sides of a 9 by 9 by 2 inch greased baking pan.

The Filling:

In a mixing bowl, beat the sugar and butter/margarine until it is light and fluffy. Mix in the egg until combined then alternately add the flour and the evaporated milk, mixing after each addition. Next add the corn syrup and the vanilla extract and mix at medium speed until well blended. Pour the batter into the crust-lined baking pan and sprinkle it with the powdered sugar. Bake it at 350 degrees F for about 25 to 35 minutes or until the cake is almost set. Do not overcook. Cool it in the pan before serving. Serves eight or nine.

JOE FROGGERS (MARBLEHEAD, MA)

During the early 1800s, local fishermen often carried barrels of a certain type of rum and molasses cookies aboard. These treats were baked by an Aunt Crease, who lived with a Revolutionary War veteran named Black Joe near the edge of a pond in Marblehead. They sometimes converted their home into a tavern where Aunt Crease would cook, Joe would play the fiddle, and the frogs in the nearby pond would croak along in time. Her famous cookies became known as Joe's Froggers and later as Joe Froggers … and are still a Massachusetts tradition.

Wha' Cha' Need:

Four mixing bowls
Plastic wrap
Rolling pin/board
Cookie sheet

½ cup of hot water
½ cup plus one tablespoon of dark rum
One cup (2 sticks) of butter
Two cups of sugar
Two teaspoons of baking soda
Two cups of unsulphured dark molasses
About seven cups of flour
One tablespoon of salt
One and ½ teaspoons of ginger
One teaspoon of cloves
One teaspoon of allspice
½ teaspoon of freshly grated nutmeg

Wha' Cha' Do:

Combine the hot water and rum in small bowl. In large bowl, cream the butter and sugar together. Combine the baking soda and molasses in a third bowl, and in a fourth combine seven cups of flour with the salt, ginger, cloves, allspice, and nutmeg. Blend the water/rum mixture into the creamed butter/sugar mixture. Add the baking soda/molasses mixture and the dry ingredients alternately; and blend it all together. If the dough gets too stiff add some water; if it is not stiff enough add more flour. Divide the dough into three balls, wrap them in plastic wrap, and chill them thoroughly. Preheat your oven to 375 degrees F. Sprinkle a board with the remaining flour and roll the dough out to about ¼ inch thick, but avoid too much rolling. Cut it with a two-inch diameter cookie cutter or the rim of a glass. Bake them on a greased cookie sheet for about ten minutes. Makes around eight dozen Froggers!

KEY LIME PIE (KEY WEST, FL)

The first written recipes for this official dessert of the Florida Keys did not appear until the 1930s, but Conchs were enjoying it long before then. Some claim it was invented by local fishermen, but others maintain it was created in the late 1800s by a cook for the salvager "Rich Bill" Curry, Florida's first self-made millionaire. Most agree that it came to be because of the shortage of fresh milk and the lack of refrigeration in the Keys until completion of the overseas highway. Local cooks had to rely heavily upon the canned and sweetened condensed milk that Borden invented in the 1850s. Fortunately, they discovered that Key Lime juice turned condensed milk and egg yolks into a custard-like filling, and Key Lime Pie was born ... but please don't color it green!

Wha' Cha' Need:

Mixing bowls
Nine-inch pie plate
Mixer

The Shell:
16 Graham cracker, crushed
Three tablespoons of sugar
¼ pound of margarine or butter

The Filling:
Four large or extra large egg yolks
One (14 ounce) can of sweetened condensed milk
½ cup of fresh key limejuice (about 12 key limes)
Two teaspoons of grated lime peel, green portion only
Whipping cream for garnish (optional)

Wha' Cha' Do:

The Shell:
Mix all of the shell ingredients together and press them into a nine-inch pie plate. Bake it in a preheated 350 degree F oven for 10 to 12 minutes until lightly browned. Place the shell on a rack to cool.

The Filling:
Beat the egg yolks until they are thick and turn light yellow. Do not over mix. Turn off the mixer and add the sweetened condensed milk. Turn the speed to low and mix in half of the limejuice. Once this limejuice is incorporated, add in the other half of the juice and the zest, continuing to mix until blended (just a few seconds). Pour the mixture into the pie shell and bake it at 350 degrees F for 12 minutes. Garnish with a dollop of whipped cream or topping. Serves eight.

MACKINAC FUDGE (MACKINAC ISLAND, MI)

Native Americans regard Mackinac Island as a sacred place, and the home of the Great Spirit, *Gitchie Manitou*. Strategically located in the Great Lakes, it has long been a center for trade … but today, Mackinac Island is known for its: towering bluffs, Grand Hotel, lack of private vehicles, lilacs, and of course, famous fudge. (This recipe is included here with the blessing of Gitchie Manitou, of course)

Wha' Cha' Need:

Heavy saucepan
Electric mixer
Fudge pan

Basic Recipe:
½ cup of milk
½ cup of butter
½ cup of firmly packed brown sugar
½ cup of granulated sugar
1/8 teaspoon of salt
One teaspoon of vanilla extract
Two cups of confectioners' sugar
½ cup of chopped nuts (optional)

Wha' Cha' Do:

Mix the milk, butter, brown sugar, granulated sugar, and salt in a heavy pan.

For peanut butter fudge:
Reduce the amount of butter to ¼ of a cup and add ½ cup of peanut butter.

Cook it over medium heat until boiling. Boil it for exactly six minutes, stirring constantly. Remove it from heat and add the vanilla extract and confectioners' sugar.

For chocolate fudge:
Add ½ cup of cocoa along with the confectioner's sugar to the basic recipe.

Beat it with a mixer until it is smooth and thick, then add nuts (if desired). Pour it into a buttered pan and freeze it for about 20 minutes before cutting it into pieces. Makes about one pound of fudge.

NANAIMO BARS (NANAIMO, BC)

Most of us have heard about biker bars, and some of us have visited our share of waterfront bars, but what exactly is a Nanaimo Bar? The origin of this layered confection seems to be veiled in the mists of time, and there are lots of theories. About the only thing that most of them have in common is the town of Nanaimo in British Columbia.

Wha' Cha' Need:

Double Boiler
Eight-inch square pan
Mixing bowl

The Bottom Layer:
½ cup of unsalted butter
¼ cup of sugar
Five tablespoons of unsweetened cocoa powder
One egg, beaten
One and ¾ cups Graham cracker crumbs
One cup of sweetened coconut flakes
½ cup of almonds, finely chopped

The Second layer:
½ cup of unsalted butter
Three tablespoons of cream
Two tablespoons of vanilla custard powder
Two cups of icing sugar

The Icing:
Four ounces of semisweet chocolate
Two tablespoons of unsalted butter

Wha' Cha' Do:

The Bottom Layer:
Place the butter, sugar and cocoa powder in double boiler over barely simmering water and stir occasionally until it is melted. Next add the beaten egg and stir to cook and thicken. After doing so, remove it from the heat and stir in the Graham cracker crumbs, coconut flakes, and chopped almonds. Press it firmly into an un-greased eight-inch square pan and chill.

The Second Layer:
Let the unsalted butter come to room temperature before mixing it together with the cream and custard powder in a bowl. Gradually beat in the icing sugar until the mixture is light and fluffy, spread it over the bottom layer, and chill.

The Icing:
Melt the semisweet chocolate and butter in the top of a double boiler over barely simmering water, stirring to combine. Cool this mixture to room temperature then spread it evenly over the second layer using a spatula. After it has chilled, cut into bars. Makes 16 to 24 bars.

SPOTTED DOG (ENGLAND)

Variations of this traditional English dessert date back to 1847. It is basically a pudding made from suet pastry that is "spotted" with dried currants or raisins. It was traditionally boiled or steamed in a bag, but these days it is often baked. An Irish version is like sweet soda bread, and sometimes called "railway cake."

Wha' Cha' Need:

Mixing bowl
Clean (pudding) cloth
Large cooking pot

A pinch of salt
¼ cup of shredded suet
½ cup of self-rising flour
Two tablespoons of sugar
½ cup of dried currants or raisins
Water

Wha' Cha' Do:

Mix the salt, shredded suet, flour, sugar, and dried currants/raisins together, then add just enough cold water to make a firm dough. Form the dough into a cylinder that is about eight inches long, and place it onto a clean (pudding) cloth that has been wrung out in boiling water and sprinkled with flour. Roll it up in the cloth and tie the ends tightly, but leave room for expansion. Place it into a pan of boiling water, cover, and boil it for about two hours. Turn the pudding out onto a warmed dish and serve. Serves one.

STICKY TOFFEE PUDDING (SCOTLAND)

Scotland is the home of some of the world's finest single malt whiskey; strange musical instruments that must be squeezed to produce even stranger sounds; sporting events which involve the tossing of boulders, logs, and livestock; the royal and ancient game of golf; and of course sticky, toffee pudding. I have no idea why the latter is called pudding, since it is really more like a moist cake.

Wha' Cha' Need:

Heatproof bowl
Seven-inch baking pan
Saucepan

The Pudding:
One cup of dates, pitted and chopped
One teaspoon of baking soda
One cup of boiling water
Two tablespoons of butter
One cup of soft brown sugar
Two eggs
One and ½ cups of self-rising flour, sifted

The Toffee Sauce:
One cup of soft brown sugar
¾ cup of light whipping cream
½ teaspoon of vanilla extract
Two tablespoons of butter

Wha' Cha' Do:

The Pudding:
Mix the dates and baking soda in a heatproof bowl. Pour the boiling water on top and put it aside. Cream the butter and sugar until it is pale, and add the eggs one at a time, beating well after each. Gently fold in the sifted flour, stir in the date mixture, and pour all of it into a lightly buttered seven-inch

pan. Bake it in a preheated 350 degree F oven for roughly 30 to 40 minutes, or until an inserted toothpick comes out clean. Serves six.

The Toffee Sauce:
Combine the brown sugar, cream, vanilla, and butter in a saucepan, bring it to a boil while stirring then simmer it for five minutes. Cut the pudding into squares and place each square onto a warmed plate. Pour some of the hot toffee sauce over each square and serve it with fresh cream or whipped topping.

WHOOPEE PIES (PENNSYLVANIA)

This regional dessert consists of two chocolate hemispheres held together with icing, and is also known as "gobs." This rather odd name probably came from the picture of a sailor that was printed on the packaging of the first company to produce them commercially. Please do not get whoopee pies confused with whoopee cushions, however.

Wha' Cha' Need:

Mixing bowls
Parchment baking paper
Plastic wrap

The Hemispheres:
Chocolate cake mix
One cup of water
½ cup of vegetable oil
Three eggs
One cup of flour

The Icing:
Two sticks of margarine
One teaspoons of vanilla extract
One cup of Crisco
Two teaspoons of milk
Two pounds of confectioner's sugar

Wha' Cha' Do:

The Hemispheres:
Add the water, vegetable oil, eggs, and flour to the cake mix. Spoon into small round mounds (each about two and ½ inches in diameter) on parchment baking paper. Bake them at 350 degrees F for ten minutes or until they are firm.

The Icing:
Beat the icing ingredients together for at least 20 minutes, then refrigerate. After the hemispheres have cooled, spread icing over the flat bottoms of pairs. Wrap in plastic wrap to store. Makes about two or three dozen pies, depending upon their size. *Whoopee!*

DON'T DRINK THE WATER!

Use of alcohol aboard early vessels was simultaneously a blessing and a curse. Fresh Water had a tendency to go bad quickly due to bacterial growth. Coffee and tea were used to disguise the rancid water, and alcohol was added to hopefully kill at least some of the resident bacteria (see the Royal Navy Grog recipe in this Chapter). The unpasteurized ale of the day also spoiled rapidly, so devoted crewmembers felt that it was their duty to consume it all before this occurred.

Rum is often associated with the British Navy, but Her Majesty's Army preferred gin. Royal Navy officers could instead drink a special type of Port wine that was fortified with grape brandy to make it more stable during long voyages. Until abolished by a very unpopular Navy Secretary, alcohol rations on United States Navy ships were just as often bourbon or other types of whiskey as they were rum. One reason that rum was popular aboard many ships of the day was because it is made from fermented molasses, and was relatively inexpensive.

The consumption of rum aboard many pirate ships tended to be somewhat less regulated than on board naval vessels, and this led to their downfall on several occasions. One well-known example of this was the capture of the pirates Anne Bonny and "Calico Jack" Rackham, whose crew was simply to drunk to fight.

BAHAMA BREEZE (THE BAHAMAS)

To prove that even I can be politically correct, here is a fruit-loopy drink recipe for sissies and lily-livered landlubbers. The most dangerous thing about this non-alcoholic libation is the risk of brain-freeze if you swill it too fast.

Wha' Cha' Need:

Blender

Two cups of ice
One banana, sliced
½ cup of coconut cream
Two and ½ cups of pineapple juice
One cup of strawberries, sliced (optional)

Wha' Cha' Do:

Combine all of the above ingredients in a blender, and puree them until the mixture is thick and smooth. Pour into glasses and garnish with strawberry slices (if ye so desire). Serves six wimps.

EL MOJITO (CUBAN CANE FIELDS)

Cuban field workers were provided with large barrels of sugar cane juice called *guarapo* to drink after hot days. On Saturday nights, some plantation owners spiked their guarapo with an early form of rum called *aguardiente*. The workers began adding a type of mint leaf called *yerba buena* to the barrels for more flavor. The best mojitos are made with fresh yerba buena, but if you cannot find any you can use peppermint or spearmint leaves. A classic mojito should be very sweet!

Wha' Cha' Need:

Tall glass

Three teaspoons of sugar
Juice of ½ lime
Fresh yerba buena or mint leaves
One ounce of light rum
Ice cubes
Angostura Bitters (optional)
Soda water

Wha' Cha' Do:

Put the sugar and limejuice into a tall glass. Crush a few fresh yerba buena (or mint) leaves into the sugar and limejuice. Add the rum and ice cubes, and some recipes also call for a couple drops of angostura bitters. Fill the glass with soda water and serve with a sprig of fresh mint. It might look kind of murky, but it taste great! Serves one.

GINGER RUM (LAHAINA, HI)

Legend says that seafarers used to rattle vanilla beans in empty rum bottles to attract whales to their vessels, and follow these migrating mammals to what we now know as the Hawaiian Islands. Sugar cane grew well on Maui long before there were tourists coasting down the slopes of Haleakala on mountain bikes, and in the 1800s Lahaina was a popular port for mariners in search of whales, demon rum, and willing women (although not necessarily in that order). This became such a problem that on the 7th of December in 1827, the island chiefs passed laws against rum and prostitution. Local businessmen convinced the chiefs to repeal the laws on the 8th of December in 1827.

There are three reasons why this might be the ideal sailor's drink: (1) it contains rum, (2) the motion of the vessel does most of the work, and (3) it contains rum. So what if you have to put up with a few jars rolling about the deck for a while?

Wha' Cha' Need:

Large glass jar or jug
Small serving glasses

Lots of light rum
Fresh ginger

Wha' Cha' Do:

Fill a large glass jar halfway with fresh ginger, pour light rum to the top, and put the lid on it. Let it stand for about two weeks and roll the jar two times each day. After several weeks the rum turns golden, which means that it is ready to drink. Serve straight in small glasses. By the way, did I mention that it contains rum?

GLÖGG (SCANDINAVIA)

Contrary to what you may have heard, the name of this beverage does not come from the sound that it makes while being poured out of containers, but from the Swedish verb *glodga* which means "to mull." It is popular among Scandinavian cultures around Christmastime, but you can also drink it at other times of the year. Just make sure that you follow the proper procedures if you are in Scandinavia. No matter how thirsty you may be, never touch your glass until one of your hosts raises theirs in a toast to all. Then everybody should reply to their "skål" by simultaneously answering with a "skål" of their own. But don't drink yet! Instead, first tilt your glass toward your host or hostess then take a modest sip. Do not chug down the entire amount and do not take the bottle when you leave, or you just might be making a glögg sound as you sink in the nearest fiord.

Wha' Cha' Need:

Large saucepan
Small serving cups

One and ¼ cups of water
One teaspoon of cardamom
Five cloves
Two cinnamon sticks
¼ cup of raisins
Ten almonds
½ to ¾ cup of sugar
Two bottles of red wine
One and ¾ cups of brännvin (or vodka)
¾ cup of port wine

Wha' Cha' Do:

Stir the spices, raisins, and almonds into the water, and boil the mixture for about five minutes. Remove it from the heat, let it stand for half an hour, and strain off the spices. Mix in the sugar until it is all dissolved. Next add the port wine, the red wine, and the brännvin (or vodka) and heat it up. Serve in mugs or small cups with almonds and raisins on their bottoms.

GROG (ROYAL NAVY)

Grog was supposedly named after British Admiral Vernon, who was nicknamed "Old Grog" because he often wore coats made out of a coarse fabric called grogram. He ordered that his crew's rum ration be diluted with water to prevent drunkenness, which made him extremely popular. Grog was typically made in barrels, and rationed out to crewmembers. (Recipe courtesy of the Royal Navy shown here)

Wha' Cha' Need:

A mug

One ounce of rum
Eight ounces of water

Wha' Cha' Do:

Mix the rum and the water together. Pour it into a mug. A later recipe added the juice of half of a lime to prevent scurvy (thus originating the nickname "limey" for Royal Navy sailors), and one or two teaspoons of sugar. Serves one bloke.

REAL MAI TAI (SAN FRANCISCO, CA)

When Victor Bergeron gave the first ones of these to his friends from Tahiti back in 1944, they said *mai tai roa ae*, which means "out of this world!" The original Mai Tai recipe does not contain either orange or pineapple juice, but this once-proud drink devolved into today's concoction of fruit-juices served under a tiny parasol. But we purists know that pretenders made with any juice (except for limejuice) are not true Mai Tais. Here is the real recipe, courtesy of Trader Vic.

Wha' Cha' Need:

Serving glass

One ounce of light Jamaican rum
One ounce of dark Martinique rum
½ ounce of Orange Curacao
½ ounce of orgeat syrup
Juice of one fresh lime
Shaved ice
Sprig of mint

About Orgeat Syrup:
First of all, it's pronounced "or-zat" for some odd reason. Second, it may be hard to find, but you can make your very own reasonable substitute by: (1) combining equal parts of water and sugar, cooking this mixture over medium heat until the sugar is dissolved and letting it cool, then (2) combining two tablespoons of that cooled mixture with ¼ teaspoon of almond extract to make your orgeat syrup.

Wha' Cha' Do:

Mix all of the above ingredients and serve it over shaved ice with a sprig of fresh mint (but no tiny parasol). Serves one thirsty Trader.

SYLLABUB (ANONYMOUS)

Some recipes really ought to remain anonymous. There are three basic types of syllabubs:
whipped, everlasting, and from the cow. The
first two are made by floating whipped cream
upon sweetened wine, while making the last
one properly requires access to a live milk cow.
Here is a recipe for the latter, in case you ever find a bovine stowing away in
the wine cellar of your vessel. (Since nobody will claim responsibility for
this concoction, it must be English)

Wha' Cha' Need:

Large bowl or bucket
Serving goblets
Live milk cow

Two cups of medium-dry sherry
Two cups of mediocre port
Eight teaspoons of sugar
Two quarts of fresh milk
One whole nutmeg

Wha' Cha' Do:

Combine the sherry, port, and sugar in a very large bowl or an extremely
clean bucket. Squirt about two quarts of milk directly from the cow into the
bowl or bucket. Pour the mixture into goblets and top each with lightly
grated nutmeg. Serve while it is still warm (about 103 degrees F). Serves
eight. *Yummy!*

Note—If you or any tasteless guests happen to be from Staffordshire, use
four cups of cider and one cup of brandy instead of the port and the sherry
… and increase the amount of sugar to five tablespoons.

TROPICAL ICED TEA (THE TROPICS)

I realize that sooner or later you will no longer be chosen to be the "Designated Drunk," because nobody's luck lasts forever. In preparation for this sad event, here's a recipe for another wussy drink that will keep you cool and wide awake.

Wha' Cha' Need:

Large pitcher
Serving glasses

Four cups of water
Four cups of iced tea
One (12 ounce) can of frozen pineapple-orange juice concentrate, thawed
Ice cubes
Fresh mint leaves for garnish (optional)

Wha' Cha' Do:

Pay attention now, because this might get tricky … Mix the water, iced tea, and thawed pineapple-orange juice concentrate together in a large pitcher. Sweeten to taste, and serve it over ice in tall glasses garnished with fresh mint leaves (optional). Repeat, if needed.

VIKING MEAD (NORWAY)

Plundering and pillaging can be thirsty work, but the Vikings had a solution. So the next time you throw a party for Inga and Olaf aboard your long ship, you will probably want to whip up a few gallons of mead ... just remember to start about six months ahead of time.

Wha' Cha' Need:

Large cooking pot or kettle
Hand skimmer/strainer
Several five-gallon glass jugs
Several stoppers with tubes
Large bowl
Bottles with caps

Four to five gallons of pure spring water (not distilled)
Eight to ten pounds of raw honey (for delicate Mead)
Three teaspoons of yeast nutrient (or five tablets)
One teaspoon of malic/citric acid blend
Five to seven ounces of sliced fresh ginger root
¼ teaspoon of fresh rosemary (optional)
Five to six whole cloves (optional)
One to two vanilla beans (optional)
Cinnamon/nutmeg (optional)
Lime/orange peels (optional)
Crushed fruit (peaches, strawberries, grapes, etc.)
½ teaspoon of clear gelatin
One packet of (champagne or ale) yeast

Wha' Cha' Do:

Heat the water until boiling. Stir in the honey, yeast nutrient, acid blend, and spices (ginger, rosemary, cloves, vanilla, cinnamon/nutmeg, lime/orange peel). Boil for another 10 to 15 minutes, skimming off the foam as needed. After 15 minutes, add the clear gelatin to clarify. After the last skimming, turn off the heat, add the crushed fruit, and let it steep 15 to 30 minutes while allowing the mead to cool and clarify. After the mead begins to clear, strain off the fruit with a hand skimmer and pour the mead through strainer funnel into a sterilized five-gallon glass jug. Let it cool to room temperature for about 24 hours. Afterwards, warm up a cup of mead, stir in a packet of Champagne or Ale yeast, and let it sit for five to 15 minutes to let the yeast start to work. Add this mead/yeast mixture to the jug and swirl it around to add oxygen. Place a stopper and run-off tube into the jug, with other end of the tube in a large bowl to capture any blow-off.

Let the mead rest undisturbed for seven days in a cool, dark place. After initial fermentation slows down and mead begins to settle, siphon off the good mead into a sterilized jug, leaving all of the sediment in bottom of first jug. Attach a stopper, tube, and airlock to this second jug. After four to six months, the mead should clear. If more sediment forms on the bottom during this time, siphon off the good mead again into another sterilized jug. To add carbonation when bottling, stir in either ¼ teaspoon of white sugar per 12 ounce bottle, or ½ to one pound of raw honey per five gallons of mead (dissolve the honey first in a small amount of mead or water). Makes about five gallons. Consume that much mead and you will probably want to go out and pillage a village (or perhaps two).

WASSAIL (ENGLAND)

As every proper (and improper) Englishman knows ... when your valiant ship is afire and you are about to be boarded, when things look bad and all seems lost, when the very last glimmer of hope has faded, and after all rescuers disappear over the horizon ... you can always wassail! Its weird name comes from the Old English toast *wes hál*, that means "be in good health," and to which the proper response was "drink-hail!" This spiced punch is traditionally drunk at Twelfth Night and at Christmas celebrations, but you can drink it anytime you want!

Wha' Cha' Need:

Baking pan
Large saucepan
Strainer
Punch bowl
Punch cups

Ten very small apples
Ten teaspoons of brown sugar
Three whole cloves
One large orange
Two bottles of dry Madeira
½ teaspoon of grated nutmeg
One teaspoon of ground ginger
Three allspice berries
Two or three cinnamon sticks
Two cups of sugar
12 to 20 pints of cider according to the number of guests
One cup of brandy (or as much as you like)

Wha' Cha' Do:

Core the apples and fill each of them with a teaspoon of brown sugar. Place them into a baking pan and cover the bottom with 1/8 of an inch of water. Insert the cloves into the orange about ½ inch apart. Bake the orange with the apples in a 350 degree F oven. After about 30 minutes, remove the orange and puncture it in several places with a fork or ice pick. Combine the Madeira, nutmeg, ginger, allspice berries, cinnamon sticks, sugar, and cider in a large saucepan and heat slowly without letting it comes to a boil. Strain the wine and spice mixture, and add the brandy. Pour it into a punch bowl, float the apples and orange on top, and ladle it while hot into punch cups. Serves 15 to 20 wild wassailers.

SO YOU WANT TO BE A PIRATE?

If you have made it this far through *Captain Bucko's Galley Slave Cookbook*, you know more than most of your oar-mates. You also hopefully have a better appreciation for how much the waters of the world have affected how we live (and what we eat). As we promised in the beginning, you will not find a lot of this information in boring "land-lubber" cookbooks, which is one thing that makes them so darn boring.

Right about now, many of you are probably thinking, "Now that I have all these authentic nautical recipes, we can throw a party! We'll all dress up like pirates, we'll rent talking parrots, we'll sing sea shanties and tell salty jokes, we'll say *Arrrh* a lot, and then we'll ..."

Belay that, matey! Just because you can now cook like a pirate does not mean that you are quite ready to pretend to be one. Perhaps we had better spend a bit more time describing what life was really like back in those days. Read on.

Life afloat in early times was not quite as luxurious as it is today. Those aboard lived in cramped (and often filthy) quarters, fresh food quickly spoiled or became infested, and rats gnawed upon everything including the vessel's hull. So why in the world did folks back then put themselves through such misery? Thirst for a better life or adventure were just some of their reasons.

Most who chose to go to sea did so at a young age merely because a life at sea required stamina and dexterity that older men no longer possessed. Crewmen hauled on heavy lines, climbed aloft to handle sails in calm or stormy seas, and manned bilge pumps for hours upon end. They spent weeks, months, and even years away from home. They weathered storms, tried to avoid uncharted shoals, and worried about having enough food and water to reach their next port of call.

Some of those crewing naval vessels did so against their wishes. One common practice, especially in England, was to fill crews that were short-handed due to desertion or lack of skilled seamen by pressing landsmen into service. Whether pressed or not, many common seamen found life aboard early Navy ships to be relatively deplorable. Wages were low, widespread corruption affected both the quantity and quality of food, and mistakes or infractions were cruelly punished.

Until 1856 when most maritime countries signed the Declaration of Paris, many governments augmented their navies by issuing *Letters of Marque* to privateers, which permitted them to "legally" plunder enemy vessels. But when these same governments no longer needed their services, a substantial number of privateers became unemployed. Some of them turned to piracy, just because the prospects of becoming wealthy seemed preferable to begging or starvation. And while privateers turned over their spoils of battle to the governments that licensed them and their shares tended to be rather paltry, pirate crewmembers all got shares of the booty and even elected their own captains.

In several parts of the world, people became pirates out of economic necessity. When the fishing industry on the southeastern coast of China and the logwood industry in the Honduras collapsed, some local fishermen and loggers turned to smuggling and piracy. But others who became pirates did not choose to do so. When pirates captured a ship, those aboard who lacked any seamanship skills were often put ashore or killed, while able-bodied seamen and those possessing required skills (e.g., surgeons, musicians, carpenters) were often forced to join the pirate ships' crews. In fact, many of the Caribbean pirates during the so-called "Golden Age of Piracy" were such *forced men*.

The "fashion police" did not patrol most pirate ships back then. While at sea, crewmembers typically wore one outfit until the garments were no better than rags. In fair weather seamen favored short jackets of heavy blue or gray cloth called *fearnoughts*, whereas in foul weather they often wore canvas coats. To protect themselves from the sun they wore scarves, tri-cornered hats, or caps. Their shirts were frequently plain or checkered, and they often wore *petticoat breeches* (i.e., canvas trousers cut several inches above the ankles and coated with tar to make them waterproof and deflect sword blows).

When ashore some pirates dressed like gentlemen, wearing knee breeches, stockings, embroidered waistcoats, lace-trimmed shirts, and shoes with silver buckles and high heels. A few even wore powdered wigs or ornate jewelry. They acquired such fashionable items as shares of booty taken from captured ships. Some pirates even dressed like gentlemen at their own hangings. One of the best-dressed pirates was *Black Bart*, who wore a rich crimson damask waistcoat and breeches, a red feather in his hat, and a gold chain with a diamond cross around his neck.

During the 17th and 18th centuries, the average pirate roaming the Caribbean was in his twenties, and very few plied their trade for more than ten years. Even the famous ones like *Blackbeard* and *Captain Kidd*, were pirates for only two or three years, and very few lived long enough to enjoy their ill-gotten wealth. So, are you really sure that you want to be a pirate?

—**Captain Bucko**

OTHER RESOURCES

Books:

Greg Atkinson, *West Coast Cooking*, 2006

Lora Brody, *The New England Table*, 1998

James Burney, *History of the Buccaneers of North America*, 1816

Daniel Defoe, *A General History of the Pyrates*, 1972

John Demers, *Caribbean Cooking*, 1997

Ray Dunn, *20,000 Gallons of Chowder*, 1999

Richard Hooker, *Book of Chowder*, 1978

Roger Paul Huff., *Captain Bucko's Nauti-Words Handbook*, 2004, iUniverse

Charles Johnson, *A General History of the Pyrates*, 2006

Deanna J. Jones, *Life in a Man's World: Mary Read*, 2006

Connie C. Kanter, *The Cruising KISS Cookbook II*, 2005, Sailco Press

Jean Kerr with Spencer Smith, *Mystic Seafood*, 2006

Kay Pastorius, *Cruising Cuisine*, 1997

Robert C. Ritchie, *Pirate*, 2006

Kim Severson and Glenn Denkler, *The New Alaska Cookbook*, 2001

Elizabeth Wheeler & Jennifer Trainer Thompson, *Feasts Afloat*, 2000

Ann Wilson, *The Galley Collection*, 1998, Tiller Publishing

Web Sites:

A Taste of Nova Scotia. http://www.hgtv.com/hgtv/ah_recipes_other/article/0,1801,HGTV_3186_1958329,00.html

Cajun Recipes. http://www.cajungrocer.com/recipes-c-1170.html

Cajun Country Recipes. http://www.labellecuisine.com/Cajun%20Country/cajun_country_recipes.htm

Caribbean Recipes. http://www.caribbeanchoice.com/recipes/main.asp

Caribbean/West Indian Recipes. http://swagga.com/recipe.htm

Heart of New England Recipes. http://www.theheartofnewengland.com/food.html

Jamaican Recipes. http://www.islandflave.com/recipes/jamaica.html

Nautical Appetizers. http://www.cdkitchen.com/recipes/recs/311/NauticalAppetizers69542.shtml

Nautical Living. http://www.nauticalaccessories.com/recipes.php

Nautical Nellies Recipes. http://www.cdkitchen.com/recipes/recs/311/NauticalAppetizers69542.shtml

Nautical Themed Recipes. http://www.nauticalaccessories.com/recipes.php

New Brunswick Recipes. http://www.new-brunswick.net/new-brunswick/recipes.html

New England Cooking. http://www.newenglandcooking.com/cookbook/

New England Food & Recipes. http://gonewengland.about.com/od/recipes/New_England_Food_Recipes.htm

New England Recipes. http://www.newenglandrecipes.com/

Madagascar Cuisine. http://www.air-mad.com/about_history.html

Pirate Recipes. http://www.hgtv.com/hgtv/ah_recipes_other/article/0,1801,HGTV_3186_1958329,00.html

Seafair Pirate Recipes. http://www.seafairpirates.org/AboutPirates/PirateRecipes/Salmagundi.htm

The Ship's Galley. http://www.katyberry.com/Dorianne/galley.html

978-0-595-44537-0
0-595-44537-3

5450604R0